Glorious Courage

JOHN PELHAM IN THE CIVIL WAR

by Sarah Kay Bierle

EMERGING CIVIL WAR SERIES

Chris Mackowski, series editor
Cecily Nelson Zander, chief historian

The Emerging Civil War Series

**offers compelling, easy-to-read overviews of some of the Civil War's
most important battles and stories.**

*Recipient of the Army Historical Foundation's Lieutenant General Richard G. Trefry Award
for contributions to the literature on the history of the U.S. Army*

Also part of the Emerging Civil War Series:

**For a complete list of titles in the Emerging Civil War Series,
visit www.emergingcivilwar.com.**

Glorious Courage

JOHN PELHAM IN THE CIVIL WAR

by Sarah Kay Bierle

EMERGING CIVIL WAR SERIES

SB
Savas Beatie
California

First edition, first printing

Library of Congress Cataloging-in-Publication Data

Names: Bierle, Sarah Kay, author.
Title: Glorious Courage: John Pelham in the Civil War of Northern Virginia / by Sarah Kay Bierle.
Other titles: John Pelham in the Civil War
Description: El Dorado Hills, CA : Savas Beatie, [2025] | Series: Emerging Civil War series | Includes bibliographical references and index. | Summary: "In Glorious Courage, historian Sarah Kay Bierle reconsiders Major John Pelham's extraordinary, if short, life by drawing on primary and other sources and her extensive knowledge of the battlefields. He deserves his place in history as he lived it, not varnished with the perspectives shoved upon him by later generations"-- Provided by publisher.
Identifiers: LCCN 2024053712 | ISBN 9781611217469 (paperback) | ISBN 9781611217476 (ebook)
Subjects: LCSH: Pelham, John, 1838-1863. | Artillerymen--Confederate States of America--Biography. | Confederate States of America. Army. Stuart Horse Artillery Battalion--Biography. | Confederate States of America. Army of Northern Virginia--Biography. | Confederate States of America. Army--Officers--Biography. | United States--History--Civil War, 1861-1865--Artillery operations.
Classification: LCC E467.1.P36 B54 2025 | DDC 973.7/42092 [B]--dc23/eng/20250124
LC record available at https://lccn.loc.gov/2024053712

Savas Beatie LLC
989 Governor Drive, Suite 101
El Dorado Hills, California 95762
916-941-6896 / sales@savasbeatie.com / www.savasbeatie.com

All Savas Beatie titles are available for bulk purchase discounts. Contact us for details. Proudly published, printed, and warehoused in the United States of America.

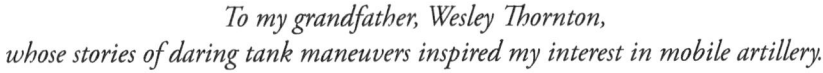

To my grandfather, Wesley Thornton,
whose stories of daring tank maneuvers inspired my interest in mobile artillery.

To my grandpa, Jerry Bierle,
who, although skilled as a sharpshooter, chose humanity instead of sniper training.

Table of Contents

Footnotes for this volume are available at
https://emergingcivilwar.com/publication/footnotes/

List of Maps

Maps by Edward Alexander

PHOTO CREDITS: Sarah Kay Bierle (skb); Central Virginia Battlefields Trust (cvbt); Culpeper Public Library (cl); John Pelham Historical Association (jpha); Library of Congress (loc); Chris Mackowski (cm); The Metropolitan Museum of Art (met); National Park Service (nps); Perry Adams Antiques (paa), Shutterstock (s)

For the Emerging Civil War Series

Theodore P. Savas, *publisher*
Sarah Keeney, *editorial consultant*
Veronica Kane, *production supervisor*
Rebecca Hill, *copyeditor*
MaryBeth Allison, *proofreader*

Chris Mackowski, *series editor and co-founder*
Cecily Nelson Zander, *chief historian*
Kristopher D. White, *emeritus editor*

Layout by Jess Maxfield

Acknowledgments

"The Pelham Project" has been a journey of research, writing, and personal growth. Significantly delayed when Covid-19 closed research libraries and archives, the book you now hold is the product of five years of thoughtful study and consideration. Many people have been involved in the process, and I'm sincerely appreciative. The following individuals have especially influenced the book project:

Ted Savas and the excellent editorial, publishing, and marketing team at Savas Beatie Publishing took on the challenge of bringing yet another Pelham book to the history shelves. Thank you.

Chris Kolakowski and David T. Dixon gave thoughtful advice, encouraging me to keep looking and follow where history and historiography led.

Chris Mackowski didn't lose faith in the project. I'm also grateful to him and his young son, Maxwell, for taking me to Kelly's Ford for the first time. I will always smile at the memory of Maxwell chasing frogs while the adults pondered the serious battle questions.

Alison Herring was there when I located the Slave Schedules (Censuses) for the Alabama counties and consistently encouraged me to ask big questions, bringing historiography to task.

Jon Tracey listened tolerantly during the winter of biography writing and talked me through the challenge to be honest and fair about history.

Jon-Erik Gilot and Sgt. David White always asked how the research was going.

My mom, Susan Bierle, encouraged hours of my research puzzles and theories, walked a few of Pelham's battlefields with me, and pushed me to "just keep writing."

Librarians and archivists who aided in the quest at Antietam National Battlefield, Anniston-Calhoun Country Public Library, Birmingham Public Library, Culpeper Public Library, Fredericksburg-Spotsylvania National Military Park, The Handley Library, The Huntington Library, Jacksonville Public Library, Jefferson County Library, Library of Congress, Library of Virginia, Martinsburg Public Library, Rauner Library at Dartmouth, Rubenstein Library at Duke University, Thomas Balch Library, Virginia Museum of History & Culture (formerly Virginia Historical Society), the Virginiana Room in Fredericksburg, Virginia Military Institute, and Wilson Library at Chapel Hill University. Any omission is accidental; there were so many excellent archives along the research journey.

Special thanks to the early readers who provided feedback and historical review: Mark Entner, Cecily N. Zander, Jim Rosebrock, Kevin Pawlak, Daniel T. Davis, and Doug Crenshaw. Thanks to John Coski for writing the foreword for the book, Tom Van Winkle and Daniel T. Davis for writing appendices, and Edward Alexander for the excellent maps. And much gratitude to the John Pelham Historical Association for granting permission to reproduce several photographs from their collection.

According to stories, Pelham's favorite cannon was a 12-pound Napoleon. (skb)

And thank you, reader, for picking up "another Pelham book." I sincerely hope you find something historically honest and something inspiring in a biography filled with glorious courage and a dash of gallantry.

$\mathcal{F}oreword$

BY JOHN M. COSKI

"John Pelham" seems so . . . well . . . wrong. So familiar is "the Gallant Pelham" that an initiate to the world of Civil War history might be excused for believing that "Gallant" was, in fact, Pelham's first name. Civil War history has more than its fair share of clichés—familiar incidents, quotations, and colorful characters—that are the shorthand of conversations among enthusiasts. Ideally, as we move from initiate toward expert, we transcend the simplistic clichés to appreciate the complexities of history and the humanity of those colorful characters. Still, it's difficult to see "Pelham" and not instinctively think, "Ah, yes, the 'Gallant Pelham,'" and to not envision a young artillerist skillfully moving his guns around the foggy fields south of Fredericksburg on the morning of December 13, 1862.

John Pelham's full humanity eludes us in part because he is a member of a small fraternity (along with J. E. B. Stuart and Turner Ashby) of mythological martyred Confederates. Their *GQ* looks and battlefield deaths (and Pelham's youthful

A Confederate memorial on the grounds of the Alabama Capitol honors soldiers of the different branches of service, including artillerists—the most famous of whom would be John Pelham (who, unlike the statue, would not have a mustache). (cm)

Pelham became a popular figure in Confederate memory. (jpha)

innocent stare) transformed them into matinee idols, then and now; they even have their own "fan clubs" (societies dedicated to the study of their short lives and shorter careers). While scholars and those societies have produced serious studies of their subjects, Pelham remains enveloped in mythology that lives on every time a Civil War buff exclaims, "Ah, yes, 'the Gallant Pelham!'"

Sarah Bierle's biography seeks to extricate John Pelham from the mythology that surrounds him and focus on what we actually know, while subjecting the mythology itself to critical analysis. Her task is complicated by the severe paucity of Pelham's own letters, which, she aptly observes, "silences" his own voice and has empowered the myth makers to fill in the silences.

Employing available primary and secondary sources, including previously undiscovered documents, Bierle's admirably clear and concise chapters review Pelham's early life, his West Point years, his maturation as both man and officer, and the military engagements that built and burnished his well-deserved reputation as a pioneer of effective horse artillery. She guides readers beyond that foggy morning at Fredericksburg and that fatal day at Kelly's Ford to other fields, famous and obscure, including what she assesses as the "height of Pelham's success as a horse artillery commander" during the Loudoun Valley Campaign. By the time you finish this book, you will have met John Pelham, perhaps for the first time.

JOHN M. COSKI *is the author of* The Confederate Battle Flag: America's Most Embattled Emblem, Capital Navy: The Men, Ships, and Operations of the James River Squadron, *and numerous other books and articles about the Civil War. In 2019, he received the Emerging Civil War Award for Service in Civil War Public History.*

John Pelham died at age 24 from a mortal wound received during the battle of Kelly's Ford. Today, a stone monument stands in his memory in the woods at Kelly's Ford battlefield. (skb)

"With a Pelham on each flank,
I could whip the world."

— *General Thomas J. "Stonewall" Jackson*

Prelude

He stares into the camera lens. Upright and poised. Jaw slightly set, but still an open and pleasant expression. Light hair combed back. Four upper buttons of his cadet uniform open. His right hand, gently fisted, rests in front of him. John Pelham of Alabama—as captured in a portrait photograph before the Civil War. Years later, a Confederate veteran described this image:

> *The inclosed[sp] is the best picture of Pelham that I have seen. It looks like he did when he first returned from West Point and also when he was killed. At other times he was thinner, because of active service. . . . A perfect picture of Pelham cannot be had, because his most remarkable feature was his eyes. In social life they were gentle and merry, 'laughing eyes;' but in the animation of battle his eyes were restless, and flashed like diamonds.*

John Pelham: son, brother, friend, artillerist, "Gallant." (loc)

Something in Pelham's expression holds the viewer's attention. Who was he? A popular internet search engine offers a quick answer: Pelham was a "soldier." True, but this young man trained as a West Point cadet for five years followed by barely two years of active military service in the Confederate cause. He only lived to age 24. There is more to Pelham's life story than simply soldier. Who was he . . . really?

In more than a century and a half since Pelham lived, numerous articles and biographies have been written about him. His death at an early age during the Confederate cavalry's zenith in the Eastern Theater and when the embattled South had time and an inclination to publicly mourn a fallen officer gave rise to stories even before his coffin arrived in his home state. After the Civil War, Pelham's place in the Lost Cause memory soared

and admirers placed him in the upper ranks of the Confederate pantheon; a youth from Alabama rode alongside the "war-gods" of Virginia: Lee, Jackson, and Stuart. His youth balanced their age. His battlefield successes contributed to theirs. But the Lost Cause hero status exacted a price—in the memory of his life, Pelham had to conform to the ideals of active veterans and later generations as they justified their view of the war. The unknown details of his life could be filled in to reflect the agenda of a retrospective Confederate memory narrative. Pelham could be their ideal young martyr because of his battlefield victories and his sudden death, but post-war chroniclers would ensure that his bachelorhood also fit their image of a legendary hero.

Pelham's experience and command during the Civil War was not all daring gallantry. He managed the logistics for the Stuart Horse Artillery, including ensuring that there were spare wheels and plenty of ammunition. (skb)

Through unfortunate circumstance, most of Pelham's own writings—particularly his letters to his family—disappeared in the early 20th Century. Whether accidental or intentional, the loss of these letters has effectively silenced Pelham. In most of the important battlefield moments of his life, his side of the story does not exist. A few official reports and military correspondence remain, but these do not contain his thoughts or feelings. Surviving letters from his West Point days, his account of the battle of First Manassas, and a few other notes to friends or acquaintances suggest that he would have penned thoughts and even feelings, making the absence of his private papers a deep loss to his family, researchers, and those crafting his memory.

With his own voice mostly vacant, others offered their primary source versions of Pelham's experiences. Contemporary accounts from peers, subordinates, and lifetime admirers emerged. People described how they saw or remembered Pelham during his lifetime . . . and, more frequently, after his death. Then secondary sources picked up the banner of Pelham's memory, usually influenced by historiographical trends and even later social movements. Finally, summary-style sources recycled the views of the secondary sources, treating opinion as fact and lessening the chance of sorting out the truth. Pelham the legend exists in popular mythology, but Pelham the man seems lost to history.

Welbourne is a historic home in Loudoun County where Pelham breakfasted at the beginning of the late autumn 1862 campaign . . . and, according to family lore and evidence, carved his name into a glass windowpane. (skb)

Across the decades, Pelham has been cast as a hero, a womanizer, an innocent, a warrior, an artillery genius, an ill-fated lad, a secessionist, and—more recently—a villain who got the death he deserved. But did any of these labels fit the man? And if some should stay in our studies and historic memory, are there others that need to be added or amended to help us understand him?

Through necessity, we are forced to see Pelham through the eyes of others. We must evaluate if those perceptions are accurate, masked by legend, or clouded with ideology. But in the moments where layers of historic varnish and propaganda are stripped away, truths need little embellishment. For example, during the Loudoun Campaign in November 1862, Pelham had a stellar moment, employing a blend of traditional and innovative horse artillery tactics which shines through the account of an observer:

> *He had been greatly annoyed during the day by a squadron of Federal cavalry which operated with great dash against his batteries, rapidly throwing forward their sharpshooters and as rapidly withdrawing them, after their muskets had been discharged, behind a piece of wood which completely hid them from view. This*

they did before Pelham could get a shot at them, and they had already killed or disabled many of his horses, when our gallant major, losing all patience, suddenly advanced with one of his light howitzers at full gallop towards the wood, where the horses were unhitched and the piece drawn by hand through the impeding undergrowth which rendered further progress of the horses impossible . . . The Yankee squadron . . . had come very quietly to a halt without the slightest suspicion that a cannon loaded with a double charge of cannister was directed upon them from a point only a few hundred yards off. All at once, the thunder of the howitzer was heard, and its iron hail swept through the ranks of the Yankees, killing eight of their number . . . wounding several others, and putting the rest to flight in hopeless stampede. Pelham and his cannoneers now emerged from the wood in a run, bringing with them many captured men and horses, and the Federal standard, amid loud shouts of applause. Before the Yankees could recover from their astonishment, the howitzer was removed, the horses were hitched to it again, and it had arrived safely at the battery.

General "Jeb" Stuart's hat and headquarters' scene would have been familiar sights to Pelham. Though he technically was not on Stuart's staff, he frequently dined and socialized with Stuart and the cavalry staff. (skb)

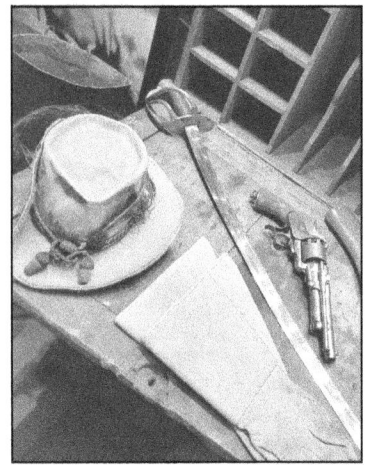

Pelham helped to transform the concept of mobile artillery on Civil War battlefields. He did not invent horse artillery, and he was not the only American officer to attempt and refine the concepts during the 1860s. However, he was one of the most successful horse artillery commanders, learning to place his cannons on the flanks of his enemy or directly in their path and then rapidly shift to another advantageous position. On the offensive or as a best defense, he added firepower to support traditional cavalry units. He used mobile artillery to screen movements or guard the rear of a column. He positioned artillery to cover the flank of infantry. Pelham brought innovation and daring to his artillery role. He does not need legend and embellishment to enhance his military accomplishments.

During his lifetime, people commented briefly on John Pelham's actions and demeanor. After his death, they wrote his story and his memory for him, adding complicated layers to the story to fit that needed mythical figure. Today, the temptation to continue the commentary about Pelham remains steady and enticing. But is it fair to him?

What if we restrained the passing of judgement and the crafting of legend for a moment? What if we could piece together a version of the truth drawing just from primary sources closest to Pelham's lifetime? What if we accepted that this fact-based version of Pelham may differ substantially from the man of legend . . . and then asked why the noticeable difference?

The steady gaze captured in Pelham's photograph stares back at us. The longer we look and the more we try to understand, the more we are confronted with the idea that when we paste labels, verdicts, and judgements on this man, we pass them on ourselves, too. Staring back at Pelham, we attempt to understand him as a boy, a man, a cadet, a soldier, a Confederate, a white Southerner. We try to see beyond the labels pinned on him in historical memory. Who was he? How did comrades see him? How did enemies fear him? How did civilians feel when around him?

Researching Pelham through primary sources bereft of imagination feels like watching someone's actions, but rarely getting to understand why. He can seem robotic because his thoughts and feelings are missing. He is silent while others speak about him. But he really lived—he had thoughts, emotions, hopes, dreams, fears, and anger. Recognizing Pelham as human before hero requires focusing on what is provided from the remaining historical record. To simply understand that—while it is possible to better understand his actions and the outcomes or consequences through primary sources and historical context—he will remain somewhat distant and unknown. A person can be observed, but never quite understood. A person can be seen in a photograph, but no words can be spoken.

In the end, this is not about telling Pelham's story where he is silent. This is about understanding what is known about his short life and sifting the long memory around his name. It is about working with the strongest primary sources and historical context. It is about knowing that Pelham keeps his secrets and coming to accept peace with that . . . out of respect for his humanity.

Alabama Home:

"He was like other boys"

CHAPTER ONE

A little one in his mother's arms, blinking and crying at the great world for the first time, has no idea of his future. Neither do his parents. Later, people beyond a family circle may remember the otherwise insignificant details of a child's birthplace once his place in history is established. On September 7, 1838, in a small wooden house near Cane Creek in Benton County, Alabama, Atkinson and Martha Pelham welcomed their third son and named him John.

One day, John Pelham's name would be in newspapers on both sides of the Atlantic. Men would enter the room that family stories marked as the place of his birth and hack wood from the walls to make relics connected to their boy-hero. But that would all be in the future, after the baby grew through boyhood, then found his place as a man in the ranks of a Confederate army that few had imagined in the 1830s.

Security and safety marked the early days and years of Pelham's life. His father, a doctor and farmer in an agriculturally developing county in northeastern Alabama, was respected in the community and looked

The sun sets near Cane Creek, Alabama, and this high ground overlooks the vicinity of John Pelham's birthplace and early youth.
(skb)

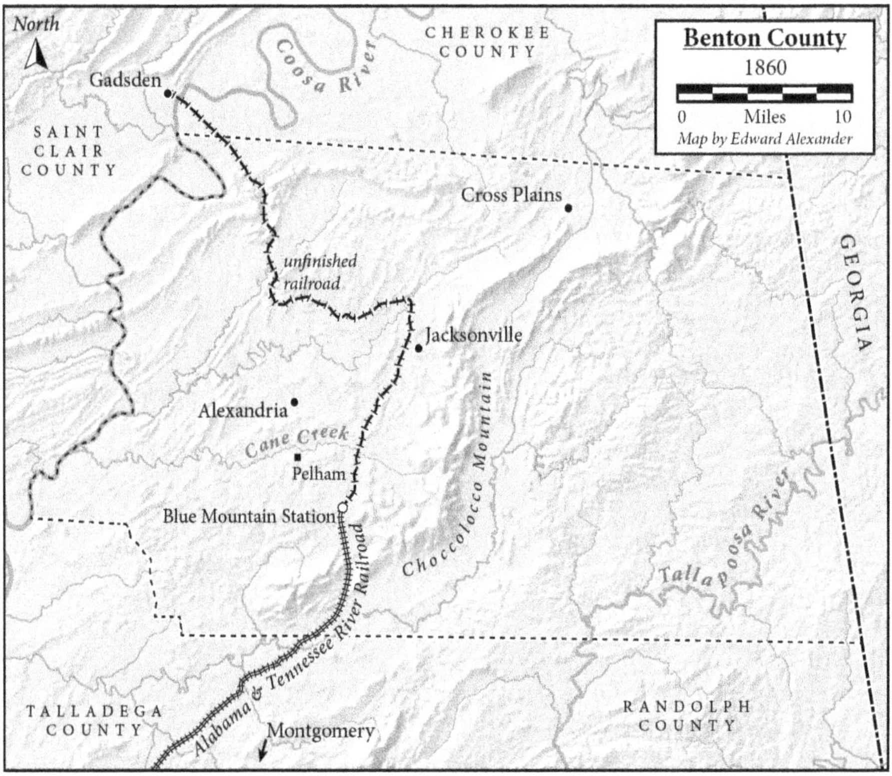

North

Gadsden

CHEROKEE
COUNTY

Benton County
1860

0   Miles   10
Map by Edward Alexander

SAINT
CLAIR
COUNTY

Cross Plains

*unfinished
railroad*

Jacksonville

Alexandria

Cane Creek

Pelham

Blue Mountain Station

Choccolocco Mountain

GEORGIA

TALLADEGA
COUNTY

Montgomery

RANDOLPH
COUNTY

BENTON COUNTY—Pelham grew up in Benton County, Alabama—but the county changed its name to Calhoun County in 1858 in memory of John Calhoun of South Carolina and his fiery, southern rhetoric.

Dr. Atkinson Pelham—John's father—was a community leader, physician, and planter. His sons accused him of not wholeheartedly supporting the secession cause at the beginning of the 1860s. (jpha)

after the physical well-being of his family. Atkinson Pelham had graduated from Pennsylvania's Jefferson Medical College in 1826, one of the few medical schools in the United States at the time. He married Martha McGhee in Person County, North Carolina, on December 22, 1833. The couple's first two sons were born in North Carolina, Charles (1835) and William (1836). Shortly before John's birth, the family moved to Benton County, Alabama, settling near Cane Creek.

Benton County—later split by politics to include Calhoun County in 1858—formed part of the southern frontier in the 1830s. When the federal government forced the removal of indigenous nations from the lower South, native lands in Alabama and Georgia were opened to white settlers who eagerly purchased land to expand their agricultural economy. Cotton made a firm foundation in that economy and with that cash crop's expansion, slavery continued and increased.

County records suggest that Dr. Pelham's medical practice kept him busy, but he also purchased land and slaves in an effort to achieve economic success for his growing family. Over the years, the family lived in Jacksonville and later in Alexandria. As his sons reached their teen years, Dr. Pelham relied on them to oversee his various farms. Though he had occasional disputes with his sons, Atkinson Pelham was remembered for his strong character and his happy family.

Martha Pelham, and likely an enslaved woman, looked after baby John as he grew, crawled, toddled, and walked. They would have cared for him through childhood illnesses and guarded him against accidents that claimed the lives of many young children in that era. Four more children were born after John. Peter (1840), Eliza "Betty" (1841), Samuel (1845), and Thomas (1847) completed the Pelham family and undoubtedly kept their mother's days busy. In later years, Martha Pelham was described as a noble and worthy woman. A few of her own letters from the 1850s reveal her worry and care for her children.

The Alabama Historical Association placed this sign in 1963 near Anniston, in Calhoun County, Alabama. The Pelham cabin is no longer standing, but the vicinity is marked along the highway with this sign. (skb)

Martha McGhee Pelham— John's mother—missed her children when they were away from home for school, work, or professions. She anticipated the times when the whole family would return to the home roof. (jpha)

As they grew, the six Pelham boys inspired the talk of the county for their pranks and outlandish adventures. They rode milk cows in a neighbor's pasture until the irate farmer told them to quit, leaving a loophole that they could ride the bull, if they wished. The boys cornered the bull, John climbed the fence and dropped onto the beast's back, and in time, tamed the bull so that Betty could ride it, too. In response to a punishment deemed unfair, the Pelham boys broke up their local school, removing all the chairs and desks, throwing the schoolbooks into the well, and "fixing" the teachers chair so it collapsed when he tried to sit down under a barrage of paper wad balls. Fistfights with neighbors occurred regularly, but the causes went unrecorded.

Fragments of family stories and recorded circumstances suggest that John Pelham may have been one of the quieter, more teachable, and responsible of the boys. He made a habit of studying diligently and came to respect a male schoolteacher from the North (the replacement for the harassed teacher). In his mother's letters, which survive from the 1850s, she writes anxiously about all the absent boys except for John, almost as if she felt she did not need to worry about the morals and character of her third son.

In his mid-teens, John Pelham spent months on one of his father's farms. Several enslaved men lived and worked the land with him. "He was like other boys had his fights, loves . . . " his brother Peter later remembered, adding, "He worked on father's farm, went fishing on Saturdays & studied the West Minister Catechism on Sunday." Perhaps young Pelham thought he would spend his life as a farmer in northern Alabama. Perhaps for a time, that is what he wanted. But new influences entered his life.

Someone—likely his father—got the idea of sending John to the United States Military Academy at West Point. At first glance, reasons for this career path look surprising. The Atkinson Pelham family did not have immediate ties to the military. Stories later entered the records that John wanted to be a soldier.

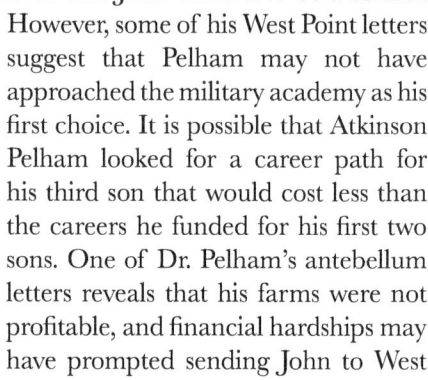

However, some of his West Point letters suggest that Pelham may not have approached the military academy as his first choice. It is possible that Atkinson Pelham looked for a career path for his third son that would cost less than the careers he funded for his first two sons. One of Dr. Pelham's antebellum letters reveals that his farms were not profitable, and financial hardships may have prompted sending John to West

Pelham brothers. (jpha)

Point where the expense of his education would be footed by the United States government.

With help and endorsement of his academic skills from a local minister, Pelham applied for an appointment to West Point. According to a reminiscence, Pelham received his West Point appointment through the influence of Senator Miles Washington Abernathy. In March 1856, he received a letter that Secretary of War Jefferson Davis had approved his appointment. It would not be the last time that Pelham and Davis exchanged correspondence or knew of each other. John Pelham wrote his acceptance and reply on March 18, 1856, and below the teenager's message, Dr. Pelham formally signed his permission for his minor son to enter military service for eight years. Enclosed with the acceptance letter, his father enclosed a doctor's note stating John was "17 years old in Sept. last, and fills <u>all</u> the physical regulations of the Circular attached to the appointment. He has my consent to enter into any engagement with [the] U.S." (Emphasis in original.)

When John Pelham committed himself to cadetship at West Point, the first chapters of his life closed. His path to fame lay far away from the banks of winding Cane Creek, the companionship of his siblings, and the guidance of his parents. The seventeen years he had spent there constituted most of his life. The experiences and lessons at home, school, and the farms of north Alabama forged John Pelham's character and influenced his decisions that would provoke controversy and launch him to fame.

But that last sunset night before Pelham started northward marked a significant change in life. If all went as planned, it would be at least two years before he saw his parents and siblings again. The threshold lay before him, and when he left home, the school of the soldier and the questions of national division would claim him forever.

The earliest known photo of John Pelham—here, he appears well-dressed and with fashionably tousled hair, perhaps hinting at the escapades he and his brothers brought to their neighborhood. (jpha)

West Point:

"I John Pelham do solemnly swear"

CHAPTER TWO

Nearly 1,000 miles north of Calhoun County, Alabama, the United States Military Academy at West Point sits at a strategic position along New York's Hudson River. In the Revolutionary War days, it had been a key defensive point for Continental forces. By the mid-19th Century, its position had acquired more theoretical value as the constructed halls, classrooms, and barracks served to teach rigorous academics and inspire the concepts of strategy, loyalties, and a sense of patriotic nationalism in the minds of the young men who arrived. For John Pelham, his five years at West Point proved an important period that influenced and reinforced the life-altering decisions he would make as civil war tore the country apart.

Pelham arrived at West Point in early June 1856, and family records indicate that he traveled through Kentucky to visit extended family during his trip northward. His mother wrote on June 15 to another family member, saying, "We had a letter from John he reached W. Point . . . seem well pleased." Academy

A modern view of the United States Military Academy at West Point from the Hudson River. (s)

In 1846, an artist created this view from the Hudson River of approaching the United States Military Academy at West Point. Pelham would likely have seen a similar scene as he arrived in 1856. (loc)

records recorded his entrance on July 1, 1856. The process of acceptance and cadetship was less rigorous than in the modern era. Young men from across the nation were appointed by congressmen and arrived at West Point over a period of a few weeks in the summer, following their acceptance. Since most young men were underage at the time of their appointments, their fathers or guardians had to legally permit them to join the military and academy.

Most cadets arrived by steamboat on the river. The scenic river with its high cliffs unfolding to reveal the castle-inspired walls of the military filled many aspiring cadets with wonder and temporarily pushed away homesick feelings. Morris Schaff, who attended West Point in overlapping years with Pelham, described the moment:

> *The boat sped on, and I heard a passenger nearby observe, 'There is West Point!' My heart beat, and at once I caught the flag crimsoning in the distance. It needs but this bit of color, the proud banner lifting and swirling out gracefully, and sinking back tenderly to the mast, to blend the scene with the thrill of its heroic associations. . . . Soon we were at the dock, and soon we were ascending the slope. . . . The road from the wharf . . . bears up the face of the precipitous bluff with a commanding grade. Approaching the summit it swings sharply to the left, around massively shouldered, lichened rocks overshadowed by native forest trees, then turns to the right, flanked by a heavy wall, and emerges near the library upon the Plain one hundred and sixty feet or so above the level of the river. The Plain, which is the counterpart of the*

This 1880s photograph shows West Point cadets drilling with a light artillery battery. (loc)

campus at universities and colleges, is as level as a floor, and has an area of forty odd acres.

Once ashore, Pelham prepared to report for the first time. His summer as a plebe had begun. Pelham joined the Class of 1861 and hoped to graduate in five years. Before and after a brief period in the 1850s, the United States military academies have followed a four-year course of academic study and military training. However, a five-year course had been ordered by Jefferson Davis—then U.S. Secretary of War, later President of the Confederacy. Pelham's Class of 1861 was one of the few subjected to the five-year rule which ended with the Civil War. Cadets were called "plebes" when they entered the academy; their first year at West Point was called the "fifth year" and subsequent years counted down until they were "first year cadets" on the eve of graduation. After graduation, the young men commissioned as second lieutenants and went into active military service—usually at forts or on the frontier in antebellum America.

A surviving piece of official paperwork shows that Pelham declared his intentions on July 19, 1856:

West Point has layers of history and buildings at the military academy. This building, called "The Ordnance Compound," was built in the 1830s or 1840s and became one of the examples of Gothic Revival design that would be copied and improved by later architects. (loc)

I John Pelham, of the State of Alabama aged seventeen years, nine months, having been selected for an appointment as Cadet in the Military Academy of the United States, do hereby engage, with the consent of my Father in the event of my receiving such appointment that I will serve in the Army of the United States for eight years unless sooner

Emory Upton hailed from New York and entered West Point in 1856; during the Civil War, he gained fame for his innovative infantry tactics and later wrote about American military policies and practices in a volume that was published posthumously after his suicide. (loc)

Edward Porter Alexander graduated in the Class of 1857 and during the Civil War would command artillery for James Longstreet's First Corps at Gettysburg. He later jotted a few brief memories of Pelham in his memoirs. (loc)

discharged by competent authority. And I John Pelham do solemnly swear that I will bear true faith and allegiance to the United States of America, and that I will serve them honestly and faithfully against all their enemies or opposers whatsoever, and observe and obey the orders of the President of the United States, and the orders of the Officers appointed over me, according to the Rules and Articles of War.

That oath was later "sworn and subscribed to, at West Point, New York, this Thirty-first day of January 1857" in front of the Clerk of Orange County, making it legally binding.

Cadets spent the summer weeks in an encampment, living in tents to simulate a military camp and schooled by upper classmen in military duties and traditions. In the autumn, Pelham started his academic studies in the Fifth Class. He ranked in the lower third of his class in Mathematics and English. He also acquired 70 demerits in his first year. At some point, he was hauled before a mock trial court for a type of hazing; the court "tried" him for reading his Bible instead of a military manual.

Limited information exists for Pelham's first two years at West Point, and his letters from these early years are missing. He finished his Fourth-Class Year—which ended in June 1858—ranking 35 in Mathematics, 39 in English Studies, and 33 in French out of a class of 52 members. His demerit record for the year stood at 92, mostly for relatively minor infractions.

Pelham's classmates in the Class of May 1861 included: Adelbert Ames, Orville Babcock, Samuel Benjamin, Charles E. Cross, Justin E. Dimick, Henry A. DuPont, Charles E. Hazlett, Mathis W. Henry, Hugh J. Kilpatrick, and Emory Upton. Though not in his class, Pelham would have been acquainted with other young men who would gain fame or infamy in the 1860s. For example, Edward Porter Alexander (Class of 1857), Stephen D. Ramseur (Class of 1858), Wesley Merritt (Class of 1858), Alonzo Cushing (Class of June 1861), Patrick O'Rorke (Class of June 1861), and George A. Custer (Class of June 1861). Multiple classmates remembered Pelham with fondness, both in their cadet years and later as men who fought on both sides during the Civil War. Pelham gained respect and saw other perspectives as he lived and studied with young men from other parts of the country with differing views on the important topics of the times. When interviewed at age 96, Adelbert Ames recalled Pelham with kindness:

> *He was easily the most popular man of the Corps in my time. Everybody liked him. I never heard anyone say a word against him. He was that kind of man, the kind of man whom you felt instinctively, 'Here is a friend.' Not that he was the sort to put himself forward to claim attention. No; he was quiet, simple, unassuming, unpretentious. There was a reserve about him that we got to know covered an inward strength. I came to know him better than the other boys from the South because, in the Third or Fourth Class, I've forgotten which, when quarters were being re-assigned to make ready for the incoming class, he lived in my room for two weeks. I got close to Pelham, you see, and I knew the man. There was something about him that drew you to him. I suppose nowadays it would be called personality.*

Adelbert Ames, Class of (May) 1861, entered West Point in the same year as Pelham. Ames would attain the rank of brevet major general in the Union Army during the Civil War and later serve as a senator from Mississippi during the Reconstruction Era; he fondly remembered his classmate from Alabama. (loc)

While other cadets echoed Ames's assessment of Pelham, some became close friends. Thomas Rosser from Texas numbered among Pelham's confidants and trusted comrades. Both entered the academy in 1856, and according to Rosser family lore, Pelham stuffed paper in his shoes to look taller so he and Rosser would room and march together since height determined those allotments. In 1861, toward the end of his cadetship, Pelham wrote a letter to his cousin Marianna who lived in Philadelphia, sharing about his friendship with Rosser: "We have been living together for three or four years, and I feel like we are inseparable—like his presence is necessary to my happiness. . . . You must allow me to introduce him."

In 1858, Pelham looked forward to the furlough and summer visit with his family. Typically, cadets at West Point in the antebellum period only had one summer furlough and remained at the barracks for the other years. Pelham wrote to his father in March to begin the arrangements for permission and travel. His mother joyously wrote to another family member about her preparations: "But I am making arrangements for a watermelon patch for you. . . . And I am raising

Thomas Rosser and Pelham were roommates at West Point and in the same Class of 1861. A couple of years later during the Civil War, Rosser commanded cavalry and eventually rose to the rank of major general; this is a war era photograph. (loc)

In his senior year at West Point, Pelham helped organize dances at the military academy, sometimes serving as "floor manager." This sketch created by Winslow Homer and published in 1859 depicts cadets and young ladies at a West Point dance. Could Pelham be one of the unidentified cadets in the scene? (met)

chickens . . . all for you children when you come this summer." She could hardly wait, "looking ahead to the pleasure of seeing you boys all together. . . ."

Pelham departed West Point in June and spent most of his 10-week leave in Alabama. On his trip south, he may have stopped in New York City to have a photograph taken in his cadet uniform. Once home, Pelham seemed to return to his rural routines, helping with horses and agriculture and also catching up with old friends in weeks that seemed "like a pleasant dream" and left "every action[,] word & thought . . . vividly stamped upon the mind."

Girls became part of his correspondence after he returned to West Point in August 1858. He sent a letter to his brother with advice for romantic courting; whether he was entirely serious or offering tongue-in-cheek advice is difficult to judge. "Remember the best weapon for conquering women is flattery. Don't talk to them about History or Grammar, nor the Philosophy of Socrates or Zeno, but them about the Moon, spoons, the Starry Heavens, and moonlight walks. . . ." Pelham may have had a summer fling with "Miss Addie," since in the same letter he felt obligated to clarify: "If she was sincere in what she said (but I don't believe she was) I have wronged her in telling her such lies—I respected her, liked her company, but to love a lady is not in my composition, now." Instead, Pelham declared, "I now stand face to face with the stern realities of life."

Despondent over a floundered relationship or discouraged about returning to West Point, Pelham grimly faced reality, thinking, "when hope dies the man is in a bad condition. I believe it will be changed some time if not this year, and that it will affect my class." That autumn Pelham forced himself to carry on through unseasonably cold weather, sickness, the trials of a lame "Pegasus" (horse), and "the stings of furlough . . . making sad havoc upon my peace of mind" while "fearful breaches in my temper" compounded a series of forlorn (and not entirely specified) hopes.

Uncertainty and darkening hopes clouded the nation. Sectional tensions continued to rise over slavery. Popular sovereignty in Kansas had deteriorated to bloody murders as Free Soilers and Jayhawkers struggled to determine if Kansas Territory would become a slave or free state. Violence erupted in the congressional chambers. Orators and publishers were increasingly direct in the defense or opposition to slavery. West Point cadets were not immune to the tensions, but most turned to their studies and kept their political views silent or in private barrack discussions.

Mentally and academically tested, Pelham pushed on, entering his third year at West Point. By May 1859, though still ranking low in class overall, he wrote to his Pa: "I think I have got the best mark in my Section and I know my course very well — but I shall continue to study it until the Ex in order to familiarize myself with the different subjects." He apologized for causing his father to worry about his grades and gratefully acknowledged the financial support that his father sent, worrying that it caused the family difficulties. Eventually, he wrote to one of his brothers about his grades: "I came out low—lower than I expected, but I hope not lower than I deserved—and am not ashamed of it—42 in Philosophy—46 in Drawing & Painting—33 in Spanish."

With examinations finished, Pelham found it difficult to stay indoors or attend to his military duties. The early summer weather enticed him, and West Point became lively with summer visitors. Though he wrote to his mother that he intended to be a good bachelor, Pelham spent time at his barracks window with a small telescope, watching the girls touring the academy. His curiosity and inactivity soon changed as the corps headed for their summer encampment.

That year, the cadet's camp was named for a former superintendent of West Point: Robert E. Lee.

Entering his Second Year and getting closer to graduation, Pelham started thinking about what he would do when he left West Point. In December 1859, he wrote to his father that he planned to stay single for "four or five years after graduating" and offered criticism of officers who married young. Pelham envisioned a future where he did "not have to remain East very long" but he could "rough it on the frontiers for several years and learn whether Fate is propitious and in what direction Fortune showers her favors." In the cadet's mind, the future was clear and "the road I'll take" looked certain. However, in the same visionary letter, Pelham remarked on the frigid weather and claimed that "Old Bentz, the bugler, accounts for it by supposing that the Southerners won't let the South winds come North since the 'Harpers Ferry' affair." It was the first hint of sectional differences in Pelham's surviving letters, added without much further comment or reflections—just the facts of an old soldier's words. John Brown's Raid on Harper's Ferry in 1859 sparked debates and conflicts within the West Point barracks, as it did across the nation. Pelham's planned future would change, and the circumstances of new decisions rested in the proverbial winds, though he had no idea of that future as he wrote to his father.

During his time at West Point, Pelham excelled at active military exercises, especially horsemanship. He wrote to his mother in January 1860, describing their indoor riding hall. "We have heads, rings, lances and bars arranged around the Hall which we have to cut, thrust, parry and jump, each one taking his turn." Pelham was often called upon to help other cadets with their troublesome horses, leading to his injury on at least one occasion. He also enjoyed fencing and boxing, and Tom Rosser claimed, "You could see it was always fun for him."

By June 1860, Pelham had improved his class rankings from low to middle. Out of the 50 cadets remaining in his class, he held Ethics 26, Infantry Tactics 31, Artillery Tactics 31, Cavalry Tactics 19, Chemistry 33, and Drawing 40.

He started his First Year and anticipated a brief furlough to see his family and summer of encampment

John Brown, a radical abolitionist, made headlines in 1859 when he attempted to seize the U.S. Arsenal at Harpers Ferry and lead an armed slave revolt for freedom. He was apprehended, tried, and hanged, but John Brown's Raid drove sections of the United States further apart and closer to the brink of civil war. (loc)

fun, followed by one more year of academics and military studies, then graduation. By August 1860, Pelham's social life had improved since he had been elected president of the Dialectic Society and also helped to organize the summer dances, "Hops" as he and other cadets called them. Again, he thought about his future and wrote to his Pa, "I have almost changed my mind about the Dragoons. I am now inclined to prefer the Infantry." That autumn the Prince of Wales visited West Point, causing excitement among the corps. Pelham noted the occasion, remarking in a letter to his sister, "I enjoyed the Prince's visit vastly."

Even as he told his sister, "I am doing pretty well—not getting many demerits," Cadet Pelham's structured barracks world and planned future was about to change. His final months at West Point would force him to define loyalty, honor, and reconsider his service oath. These ideas had been on his mind. One day during his cadetship, Pelham signed his name across the top of a page in a French literature textbook; the poetry on that page tells of a mythical kingdom, a dying king, a prince, and the concepts of honor and love. Why he wrote his name on that page is unknown, but Pelham valued these character qualities, and his sense of honor and respect of those principles influenced his choices and his future leadership. Pelham defined some of his thoughts about honor without myth veneers or French language in a letter to his brother. Written on a cold, snowy night— probably by the glow from a lamp or candle—his words to his young sibling perhaps offer a summation of his character at West Point and ideas that would guide his actions as the planned future fell apart:

John Pelham likely had this photograph taken on his way to West Point or perhaps on a furlough. There is still much speculation among researchers when and exactly where Pelham's three known photographs were created. (jpha)

> *I do not think a man can be strictly honorable unless he is brave. If he fears and cringes to other men, he cannot fill the full definition of a man. When you leave home to enter college or other high schools you will find it much more pleasure to yourself and at the same time command greater respect, if you are not afraid of the other scholars, and that they cannot make you knuckle to them. But by all means avoid being contentious and quarrelsome, it shows a want to true courage. . . .*

Secession and Honor:
"Tendering my resignation when Alabama leaves the Union"

CHAPTER THREE

John Pelham marched in Company D of the cadet corps at West Point, a unit known for a preponderance of young men from the South. As sectional conflict boiled across the country, the young men in the barracks along the Hudson had their opinions. John Brown's Raid on Harper's Ferry in October 1859 prompted a divide among classmates according to Cadet Morris Schaff, "Many of the Southern cadets broke out into natural and violent passion, denouncing in unmeasured terms the Abolitionists, and everyone in the North who shared their antipathy to slavery." Adelbert Ames later remembered:

In those days on the eve of the Civil War, sectional feeling ran high at West Point as elsewhere. Cadets of the two sections were drawn more closely together. As a rule, political convictions were mutually respected, even to the same extent as religious convictions. Issues were too grave to discuss except in the most general and dispassionate way—if at all. No one's bearing under such circumstances was more wise, more discreet that John Pelham's.

Events at the capitol in Montgomery, Alabama, shaped history, the road to Civil War, and John Pelham's decisions in 1860 and 1861. Today, a statue of Jefferson Davis stands out front. (cm)

Charles Pelham. (jpha)

This music celebrated
secession and South
Carolina's role in leading
states to declare themselves
out of the Union. While it's not
known if Pelham knew this
song, he bragged that he was
an "ultra secessionist" and
favored the movement. (loc)

Pelham's discretion may have masked his thoughts and feelings to his classmates, but he had opinions about the issues of his day. According to his brother Charles, "We boys are all secessionists but Pa . . . [is] very conservative—we call [him] submissionists." Assuming Charles correctly understood his younger brother's views, then John Pelham knew that slavery lay at the root of the state's rights issue. Charles blithely bragged about a local hanging of an abolitionist "without Judge or Jury" and also several African Americans, presumably for running away or preaching the desire for freedom. Cadet Pelham had no part in these actions in Alabama, but his brother's callous attitude and conscious rejection of abolition considerations establishes some of the sentiment within the family.

However, West Point created an environment where young men from all parts of the United States came together. Pelham had formed friendships with Northerners—of note, Adelbert Ames and Henry DuPont. Willingly or unwillingly, Pelham probably heard arguments from his friends for the concept of a perpetual union of the states and abolition. Pelham also had an aunt, Martha Coffin Pelham Wright , and several cousins living in the New York whom he corresponded with and probably visited occasionally. The Wright family advocated strongly for abolition, suggesting that during his years at West Point, Pelham was exposed to abolitionist arguments through his aunt. People around Pelham offered different views than the state's rights opinions and pro-slavery society that he had grown up in and which his brothers strongly supported. This meant that Pelham had a choice. He did not blindly fall into the ranks of the Confederacy. There were alternate views and other options around him.

Unsurprisingly, Pelham did not change his opinions. Like many other young Southern men, he had already adopted an "us vs. them" mentality, which even friendships at West Point had not broken. In the 1830s—about a decade before Pelham was born—many Southerners shifted their perceptions about racial slavery from a "necessary evil" to viewing its perpetuation and expansion as acceptable. The argument for state sovereignty (states that could willingly join and willingly leave the Union) gained greater traction. Pelham's generation of young, white males heard arguments against the continuation of slavery and saw this as an aggression from northerners who wanted to curb the economic expansion into the west and the end of enslavement. Taking elder statemen's rhetoric to a new fiery level, this younger generation began to believe that their culture and way of life were under threat. If radical abolitionists gained political power in Congress, secession and the invocation of state sovereignty above union was presented as a viable, legal, and right option. Under this view, a state had more power than the federal government and a man's allegiance went first to his state.

Montgomery, Alabama, served as the capital of the Confederacy for its first few months. As a West Point cadet from this state still in the north, Pelham's name and pending commission were discussed in the halls of new government. (loc)

John Pelham had signed a service oath, declaring that if he received an appointment to West Point, he would "serve in the Army of the United States for eight years unless sooner discharged by competent authority." He had promised to "bear true faith and allegiance to the United States of America" and to "serve them honestly and faithfully against all their enemies or opposers whatsoever, and observe and obey the orders of the President of the United States. . . ." Like other men in the service of the United States military, Pelham would have to make a choice. Interpretations of the oath varied, depending on views regarding state sovereignty and state's rights. While it would have been unlikely for Pelham to choose a course other than the one he ultimately took, he had to make a decision that he believed was honorable. He had to make that choice right in his own mind while others around him offered concern, advice, or encouragement.

In November 1860, Abraham Lincoln, the Republican candidate, won the presidential election. Some southern states had already threatened to secede if Lincoln won, and by December, states in the Deep South, including Alabama, steered a course for disunion, state sovereignty, and forming a confederacy. From New York, Pelham followed the news and made his first decision. He wrote to his mother on December 11:

> *You may expect to see me at home by the 1st of Feb. 1861. I regret the circumstances which make it necessary but I don't see any remedy—ala. seems to be determined to leave the Union before the middle of Jan. and I think it would be dishonorable in me to withhold my services when they will be needed. It seems pretty hard that I should toil for four years & a half for a diploma and then have to leave without it. I am studying pretty hard and I think I will be higher after the coming Jan. examination than I have ever been before.*

To his father, Pelham wrote: "I don't see any honorable course other than tendering my resignation when Alabama leaves the Union, and offering my services to her. In this I have not acted precipitately, but in a manner worthy of myself, of my family, and of my section of the country." He revealed that he had already

written to A. J. Walker, a judge in the Alabama Supreme Court and a politician who had helped secure his appointment to West Point. Walker had advised Pelham to resign from the academy "immediately after Alabama secedes and tend your sword to her." The judge also promised to keep Pelham informed of the happenings of the Alabama secession convention and to aid him in getting a good appointment in the state or Confederacy's military. Pelham also assured his father that he had written to Governor Moore of Alabama. Though

This Alabama Secession Cockade symbolized the wearer's support of leaving the Union and joining the Confederacy; in the Pelham family, the boys favored secession, but their father had his doubts about the movement. (paa)

Pelham had begun to make his decision to resign and follow his home state's politics, he continued to seek council from state political leaders. Still, he closed his letter to his father, saying, "I wish you would write me as soon as you have time."

One month after Pelham wrote these paired letters to his parents, Alabama passed the ordinance of secession on January 11, 1861. The document declared the Constitution of the United States of America a "compact," and that the "State of Alabama now withdraws, and is hereby withdrawn from the Union known as 'the United States of America,' and henceforth ceases to be one of the said United States, and is, and of right ought to be a Sovereign and Independent State." The reasons for this action were listed as the election of Abraham Lincoln "by a sectional party, avowedly hostile to the domestic institutions . . . of the State of Alabama" and "dangerous infractions" of the United States Constitution which threatened the "peace and security" of the state. Having declared herself out of the Union, Alabama further proclaimed that a meeting with "the slaveholding States of the South" would take place in Montgomery "for the purpose of consulting with each other as to the most effectual mode of securing concerted and harmonious action in whatever measures may be deemed most desirable for our common peace and security."

This 1860s image is speculated to be cadets at West Point. The bonds of friendship, comradeship, and a military oath tested Pelham's resolve and forced him to contemplate a step that he could make compatible with his commitment to honor. (loc)

Already, southern cadets were resigning from West Point. Cyrus B. Comstock, an assistant professor, noted on December 26, "Recitations not very good. Two cadets from Ala resigned on account of secession. . . ." Pelham waited, even after learning about the ordinance of secession from Alabama. Incomplete collections of his correspondence from this period make it difficult to trace all his reasonings.

On February 1, 1861, Atkinson Pelham signed a note for his cadet son, directing: "In consequence of the troubled & unhappy condition of our country I hereby give my son John Pelham a cadet at the U.S. Military Academy at West Point New York permission to tender his resignation to the Superintendent or other proper officer of that Institution."

By March 1861, seven southern states had declared their departure from the Union and had formed a Confederacy, with the capital in Montgomery, Alabama. Pelham continued to wait, corresponding with political leaders. He even wrote to Jefferson Davis, former Secretary of War for the United States, now provisional president of the Confederacy, seeking guidance. As far as it is known, Davis did not answer the questioning cadet.

This road to the south dock at West Point—photographed in 1889—gives a visual of what Pelham might have seen as he descended to the Hudson River and left West Point for the last time. (loc)

Pelham desperately wanted to graduate, a theme that he clearly stated in his surviving letters. He also seemed to pause and wrestle with the concept of honor. Cadet Henry DuPont wrote to his parents on March 27 describing "great numbers of resignations every day," among the cadets from the South or with southern ties. Then he specifically wrote about Pelham: "Rosser, Pelham, & Rives, are here still and do not intend to resign until they receive official notice of their having been appointed & will then hand in their resignations so as to enable them to accept the appointments as soon as they are released from their engagements to the United States. They are in hopes that no official communication will be sent them so that they can remain & graduate, which they are naturally most anxious to do."

Around the same time, Pelham wrote to one of his abolitionist cousins, emphasizing his wish and plans to graduate and then resign. However, hints of frustration and loss of control laced part of the letter. "I am not master of my own acts at present. I have been appointed a 1st Lieutenant in the Army of the 'Confederate States of America'.... The appointment was made without my consent or knowledge. I cannot accept an appointment from them as long as I am a member of this Institution, but if I am recalled by the Authorities, I will obey it." In taking this stand, Pelham found an option to carry out his choice to follow state over nation while still holding honorable principles. He viewed taking a commission from another military entity as dishonorable while he still remained at West Point. To hold to his views about this detail, Pelham had "resisted every overture, on the part of my friends, to resign, disregarded their advice and braved their anger." With a hint of sarcasm, he added, "I had no idea I was so well supplied with friends. All seemed to vie with each other in attempting to force to me to resign" (Emphasis Original). He claimed that only his father and brothers actively supported his decision to graduate and take the diploma he had studied nearly five years to attain. In another letter to other family, he said that he had heard people were "cursing and abusing me awfully in Montgomery" for his decision.

A few days later, Pelham wrote a letter to Judge Walker, laying out his decision to stay and graduate, believing that it could be accomplished since "Mr. Lincoln does not seem to be very anxious for war, and I guess every thing will remain quiet till June. . . ." He assured Walker that he would continue to study diligently and stated that he hoped to join the "Southern Army" and he sent his thanks for Walker's influence on President Davis and the Confederate Secretary of War regarding his appointment. Pelham felt that "the army suits me better than anything else—and I feel a confidence that I can succeed in it."

In a revealing letter to his new sister-in-law, Pelham explained how his concept of immediate and forceful secession fit with the idea of national heritage: "Although I am a most ultra secessionist, I am still proud of the America Flag. I think that both sides ought, in justice to the illustrious dead, lay it aside as a memento of our past greatness and of our Revolutionary renown. I would fight harder and longer to bar the "Stars and Stripes" from every Northern battlement than for any other cause. They have no right to use it, and we should not permit them. It should be stored away. . . ." This idea follows the thought pattern from southerners that the original ideals from the nation's founding had been so corrupted by northern politicians that they had no choice except to break away and form a new country that better suited their ideas of economy, society, expansion, and enslavement.

Henry A. DuPont seemed to have been a confidant of Pelham's during the Alabamian's last days at West Point. DuPont was empathetic to Pelham's struggle and choice, though DuPont remained in United States Army uniform, eventually commanding an artillery battery and receiving the Medal of Honor for his actions at the battle of Cedar Creek. (nps)

Pierre G. T. Beauregard became superintendent of West Point on January 23, 1861, but he only held the post for 5 days, resigning to follow his home state of Louisiana into the Confederacy. (loc)

Even in the seriousness of the moment, Pelham explained his latest diplomatic step, which involved trying to befriend as many girls as possible near or visiting West Point. If rumors came true and southern cadets were detained and kept as prisoners of war, he wanted to have some allies to ease his imprisonment and advocate for him. However, to his chagrin, these flirtatious efforts had only been a "sad blunder." Pelham's other plans were about to be turned upside down, too.

As the situation in Charleston, South Carolina, headed toward war, Pelham knew that military authorities watched his every move. He worried about the implications of the unasked-for commission with his name already in the Alabama military. Would he be detained and imprisoned? Would it be better to resign early and leave? Cadet Henry DuPont leaned toward the concept of the Union, fundamentally disagreeing with Pelham, but he sensed the difficult and unprecedented position of his friend. DuPont recorded what he understood of Pelham's thoughts as he hesitated during the final days before carrying out his choice.

You do not understand the position in which Rosser and Pelham are in. They are not in the service of the Southern confederacy now, as they have not accepted the appointments; in fact, they know nothing more about it than you or I do, only having seen them in the paper. Take Pelham, for instance, and a man of nicer and more honorable feelings never lived. Some months ago the Governor of his state [Alabama] wrote to him offering him a high rank in the state forces if he would resign and come home. He would have nothing to do with it & did not even answer the letter and had not applied for any position in the confederate troops. But, like many others, they have appointed him a first lieutenant, that is, have published in the newspapers his appointment, there having been no application made for the place. He does not intend to serve in the army but will resign as soon as he graduates, which is quite right under the circumstances, as he cannot be expected to fight against his home and friends. He will, though, as an honorable man, never accept a commission from the Confederate States until he has resigned the one he holds in that of the United States. He thought that, painful as it would be to give up his diploma after having undergone so much to obtain it & the many advantages which the possession gives, that, nevertheless, if he received an official notification that his services were solicited in the defense of his home, that it would be his duty to give up his own inclinations & interests and tender his resignation & go home and accept the position offered to him, and was very glad that they did not send him any official information consequently.

John F. Reynolds received John Pelham's resignation at West Point. Reynolds would rise to the rank of major general and fall on the battlefield of Gettysburg in July 1863. (loc)

Honor emerges as a principal motive for Pelham. On April 15, one day after Fort Sumter's surrender, Pelham filled out a resignation form to be sent to the U.S. Secretary of War, Simon Cameron. In large letters at the bottom of the page, he wrote: "I have accepted no place or appointment from any state or government." Here, Pelham could satisfy his concept of honor while he carried out his choice to return to Alabama and fight for the Confederate cause that his home state had joined.

John F. Reynolds reviewed Pelham's resignation papers, including the note from his father and forwarded them with a summary of Pelham's academic standing to the Secretary of War. Official West Point records dated Cadet John Pelham's resignation to April 22, 1861. He would leave without graduating, choosing his state and the Confederacy over his academic goals and his allegiance to the United States.

In the darkness, he left the academy and headed south, hoping to avoid the authorities' detection. He departed from friends who stayed in the U.S. Army. Some understood his decision, even if they did not agree with him. Others gave it little thought, thinking Pelham was just another resigning cadet and anxious to hasten their own exit from West Point to put on their blue uniforms and see action as war seemed inevitable. From his perspective, Pelham had made the only honorable choice.

To one former classmate, Pelham would always be remembered as "alive, walking across the 'area.'" But as he departed, the Alabamian faced his own mortality and war. Saying goodbye to a fellow cadet, Pelham reportedly said, "I am going home. I shall be in two or three fights and then be killed."

Early War:
"I saw a youth"

CHAPTER FOUR

John Pelham had been close to graduating from West Point, and in Alabama, expectations ran high for his leadership skills and military prowess. Even the trip to his home state had moments of danger that probably contributed to the idea of his skills' value to the Confederacy. However, he quickly discovered that while West Point's book knowledge and drill guaranteed him a Confederate commission, he would have to refine his leadership style to earn the respect of a unit.

Leaving West Point started a journey to Alabama through a country in turmoil on both sides of the Mason Dixon Line. John Pelham and one of his best friends, Tom Rosser, traveled to New York City. According to family stories, Pelham escaped that metropolis with the help of the sympathetic brother of another cadet who had already gone south. A family account claimed that Pelham evaded detection while "pretend[ing] on the [train] cars that he was carrying dispatches from Genl Scott to New Port

Harpers Ferry became a hive of activity in the spring of 1861 as volunteers rallied and trained officers tried to drill them into a semblance of an army. (skb)

Barracks in Ky—so he first went West & soon made his way to Calhoun Co." He had made it home without permanent apprehension by U.S. authorities.

Having a son nearly complete the five-year course at West Point made Dr. and Mrs. Pelham proud. Even the circumstances of John's departure created a solid story for their family's position in the community, especially as the county recruited troops, expecting a brief, exciting war.

The 4th Alabama Regiment began recruiting a company from among the locals and "some of them had been big boys while [John Pelham] was one of the little boys at the village school." While waiting to be officially mustered in, these eager neighbors assembled and performed versions of militia drill to the patriotic delight of their families and sweethearts. Captain Woodruff invited Pelham to drill the company, and the trouble began. One of John's older brothers later remembered the scene.

In the early summer of 1861, Pelham trained new recruits to load and fire cannons, putting his West Point military training to use. (skb)

"He had an awful time trying to get them 'to assume the position of a soldier' but he finally got them line up after a fashion but some how the boys did not get along so well as they did with Capt W—and John got red in the face." The Pelham family honor seemed at stake. "I could see that the neighbors [thought] that the money spent upon John's military education was as good as thrown away." One of the family's friends, seeming anxious to repair the situation, prepared a committee of very respected citizens to bring the "Capts compliments & the request to give them a 'few West Point manuevers. . . .'" To the astonishment of all, John Pelham refused to have anything to do with the drilling. "Mother was mortified[;] Father didn't like the looks of things at all."

To cool off the situation, Dr. Pelham, Charles, and John took a walk. When finally asked why he refused to drill, John declared that "the Co had 'insulted' him . . . and almost swore at them." Dr. Pelham's temper flared, and it seemed like a county fight might be provoked at the insult to the family honor as he insisted on knowing

VOLUNTEERING DOWN DIXIE.

the details of the insult. "John . . . grew angry . . . & with suppressed rage told us that the 'volunteers' had not only repeatedly "stuck their hands in their pockets" but actually "chewed tobacco in ranks!"" The neighborly feud was avoided, but both father and brother worried John had a lot to learn about soldiering beyond the West Point parade field.

This cartoon pokes fun at Confederate recruits. John Pelham had strong opinions about the new recruits he was invited to drill and nearly caused an uncivil war in his home community. (loc)

When leaving home, Pelham offered his family a glimpse of his thinking about the coming fights and perhaps tried to prepare them that he had accepted the thought of a battlefield death. According to an eyewitness to the farewell, "his mother . . . said, 'God bless you John & bring you back safe to us.' With a smile on his face & his blue eyes sparkling he answered, 'If we win, Mama, your boy wants to come back, but if we lose, pray God to take him safe from the battlefield.'"

As Pelham departed, two young, enslaved men accompanied him. Willis and Newton lived in the shadows of the Confederate officer's story, probably looking after his horses, uniforms, and performing camp chores. Through the eyes of a white officer, Willis and Newton had a level of affection for Pelham, but after his death, they returned to Dr. Pelham with John's horses and other possessions—a sobering reminder of the realities of slavery.

John Pelham left his family home and reported to Montgomery, both the state capital and the capital

Joseph Eggleston Johnston took command of the newly formed Confederate Army of the Shenandoah that included the artillery rallying under Alburtis and Pelham's command. (loc)

This Engine House in Harpers Ferry is also called John Brown's Fort since it was where the radical abolitionist took refuge before his capture during his 1859 raid. During the Civil War, both Confederate and Union soldiers recognized the site, though with different feelings. (skb)

of the Confederacy, from January through May 1861. There, he accepted the lieutenant's commission that had been waiting for him for weeks. He was ordered to go to Virginia. According to one of Atkinson Pelham's letters, John left Montgomery on May 16, heading to Lynchburg, Virginia.

Arriving in Virginia, Pelham received orders to go north to Winchester and Harpers Ferry, where the Confederacy's Army of the Shenandoah assembled and tried to prepare for combat. Pelham would have been aware of some of the history connected to the picturesque location of Harpers Ferry: the U.S. Arsenal and abolitionist John Brown's raid in 1859. By early summer 1861, Harpers Ferry hosted a military camp that had a carnival atmosphere while professional officers disciplined eager volunteers to drill and become a useful fighting force. When Pelham first arrived in June, he briefly lodged with cadets from Virginia Military Institute who acted as drillmasters.

General Joseph E. Johnston commanded the Army of the Shenandoah, which included three artillery batteries: the Rockbridge Artillery, the Culpeper Battery, and the Alburtis Battery. Pelham's assignment made him a drill instructor for the Alburtis Battery, sometimes referred to as the Wise Artillery and named after a former Virginia governor. Organized and led by Capt. Ephraim G. Alburtis, the unit consisted of 62 volunteers, 4 old smoothbore cannons, limited gunpowder and shot, 4 battered caissons with

limbers, and 43 three horses. Alburtis was in his mid-forties, a leading citizen of Martinsburg, Virginia (now West Virginia), and suffering from bouts of ill health and back pain, seemed relieved to work with Pelham and gave him significant control of the volunteers.

Harpers Ferry was in Virginia in 1861, but by 1863, it was in the new state of West Virginia. (skb)

Pelham got to work and had better success organizing and drilling than he had experienced a few weeks prior in Alabama. His superior officers noted his ability to shape the mismatched and unsupplied unit into a force that could be used on a battlefield. It also attracted the attention of onlookers. In the words of one observer:

> *I recollect one morning . . . hearing a voice with a long and peculiar drawl drilling a squad of men. The difference in sound and pronunciation of the various orders were so marked that my curiosity was excited to know who this drill instructor was. . . . I saw a youth . . . with a fair complexion, blue eyes, smooth face, light hair, lightly built, about medium height, and remarkably sinewy. His boyish appearance, manly looks, handsome face, and soldier bearing riveted my attention as he and his long, drawling peculiar accent of the west pointer drilled the awkward squad that had been assigned to him.*

Civilian observers frequently visited the camps around Harpers Ferry, relishing the excitement of the

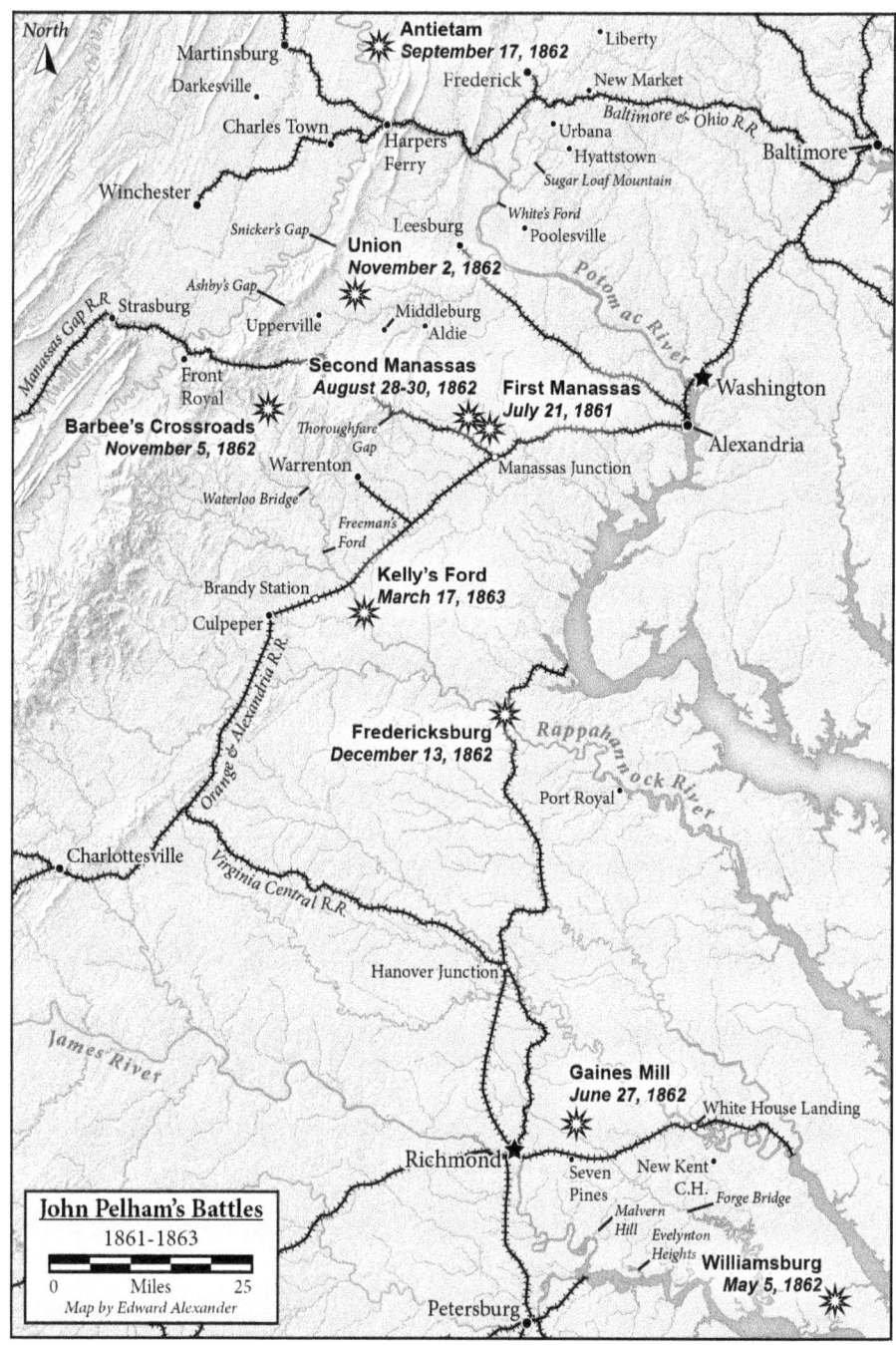

JOHN PELHAM'S BATTLES—John Pelham fought in the Eastern Theater of the American Civil War. His battlefields and areas of campaigning are located in Virginia, West Virginia, Maryland, and Pennsylvania.

martial scenes and finding their friends and loved ones in the drilling companies. The men in their various, confusing uniforms still found soldiering to be exciting and even joyous. One female visitor, Belle Boyd from Martinsburg, was taken with Lt. Pelham. Later, in 1861, she gifted him a Bible which she inscribed. Along with the note, she added poetry, including these lines: "I know thou art loved by another now, I know thou wilt ne'er be mine, But take from me still my heart's pure vow, I ask thee not now for thine." If the poetry is believable, then Boyd had feelings for Pelham which he did not return, and the hint that Pelham may have been in love with someone else has left room for speculation that Pelham may have become romantically interested in another young woman during the summer of 1861. (See Appendix A). Boyd wrote in her semi-fictional memoirs, "I fear that at this time many fond vows were exchange and many true hearts pledged between the girls of the neighborhood and the occupants of the camp; but it may be pardoned to beauty and innocence if they are not insensible to the virtues of courage and patriotism." Too sensitive to reveal specifics or firmly prove something relating to Pelham, Boyd's memory still provides insight to the scenes that artillerist drillmaster would have been surrounded by and possibly part of.

Belle Boyd resided in Martinsburg and visited friends in the Confederate camps at Harpers Ferry. She met John Pelham and eventually gifted him a Bible, though she wrote that she knew he liked someone else. Later, Boyd carried messages as an informant and spy for the Confederates and later wrote self-serving accounts of her adventures. (loc)

However, drilling and entertaining civilians only veneered the real reason these men had assembled: to fight. On July 18, 1861, Johnston issued orders, preparing the Army of the Shenandoah to march. General P. G. T. Beauregard and his Confederate force gathered near Manassas Junction on the other side of the Blue Ridge Mountains needed reinforcements, since spies had discovered that he faced the majority of the Union's army of 90-day volunteers. Captain Alburtis, Lt. Pelham, and the cannoneers of their battery turned east and toward the first test of their courage and training.

First Manassas:
"I gloried in it"

CHAPTER FIVE

The summer heat burned. Out to the front of the rising ground, battle smoke partially obscured the view, hiding the horrific carnage as two volunteer armies—mostly untrained and untested—blundered and shoved at each other with deadly volleys. Artillery batteries rolled close to each other. Federal troops advanced on Henry House Hill where the First Virginia Brigade lay impatient, their commander eyeing the advancing blue coats and his own batteries of cannon. On rising ground near Robinson's house, on the flank of Gen. Thomas J. Jackson's infantry line, Lt. John Pelham commanded the Wise Artillery. Capt. Alburtis had fallen ill, leaving the command of his guns to the young, almost West Point graduate.

Peering through his field glasses, Pelham surveyed the battle arena, choosing where to place his shots. He had plenty of targets. All of them with significant meaning or symbolism. The cannons wheeled from West Point itself, supported by United States Marines.

At the first major battle of the war, volunteers and military-trained men on both sides realized combat was bloody and likely to be more than the predicted 90 days. (skb)

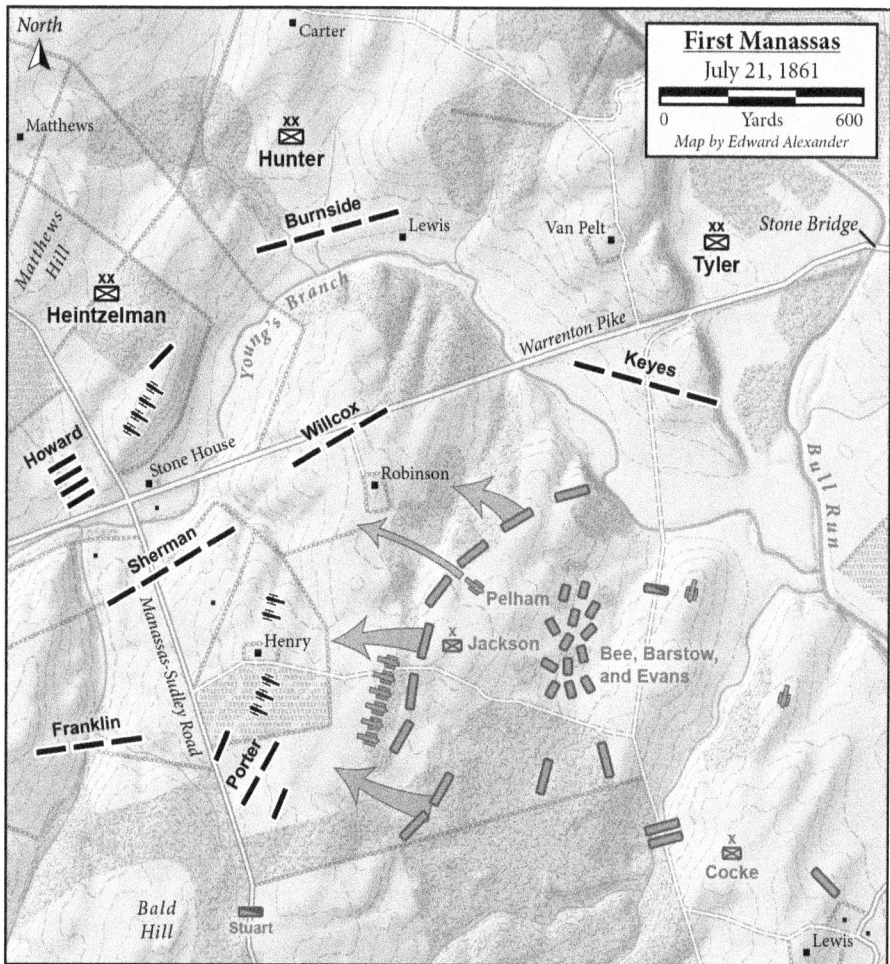

North

Carter

Matthews

First Manassas
July 21, 1861

0   Yards   600
Map by Edward Alexander

XX
Hunter

Burnside   Lewis   Van Pelt   *Stone Bridge*

XX
Tyler

Matthews Hill

XX
Heintzelman

Young's Branch

Warrenton Pike

Keyes

Howard   **Willcox**

Stone House   Robinson

Sherman

Manassas-Sidley Road

Pelham

Henry   X
Jackson   Bee, Barstow,
and Evans

Franklin

Porter

X
Cocke

*Bald
Hill*   Stuart

Lewis

Bull Run

FIRST MANASSAS—At the battle of First Manassas, Pelham's cannons formed part of the artillery line along Henry House Hill, anchoring Jackson's infantry.

Boys, his age or a bit younger or older, persuaded to enlist in the opposite cause. The flag—a symbol he had saluted for five years. On July 21, 1861, as the First Battle of Manassas unfolded, Pelham targeted them all.

Three days earlier, on July 18, Gen. Joseph E. Johnston's army maneuvered from the Shenandoah Valley toward Manassas Junction to join forces with Gen. P. G. T. Beauregard's army. While Union Gen. Robert Patterson dallied in the lower Valley, and allowed Johnston to slip away, another Union army led by Gen. Irvin McDowell headed toward the towns of Centreville and Manassas and a stream called Bull Run. Alburtis's Battery joined the line of other cannons and crews rolling eastward. They crossed

Ashby Gap in the Blue Ridge Mountains. Then, Confederate infantrymen climbed aboard railroad cars to complete the journey, while the artillery and cavalry continued the march on dusty roads. Covering nearly 60 miles between Winchester and Manassas Junction, Alburtis's Battery completed their forced march, arriving in the early morning hours of July 21.

That same morning, the Union army started a surprise march toward Sudley Springs and across Matthew's Hill, forcing the Confederate army to shift fronts as the first major battle of the war exploded. In the rear, Pelham undoubtedly heard echoes of the early fight as he confronted a command challenge. Ephraim Alburtis was sick, unable to leave his tent. If the battery went into action that day, Pelham would be the acting-captain.

Union troops gloried in their initial success. Though their ambitious march to Sudley Springs had not been executed according to the planned schedule, they still managed to drive Confederate troops across and down Matthew's Hill and back from the Stone Bridge. Hurrying reinforcements to the new front line, Gen. Thomas J. Jackson took the 1st Virginia Brigade to Henry House Hill. Jackson started bringing up artillery to form a line across the high ground, facing the guns toward the west where Confederates led by Gens. Evans, Bee, and Bartow retreated in confusion. Union troops continued to advance.

Captain Charles Griffin commanded the West Point Battery at Manassas, guns that Pelham would have been familiar with from his cadet days. (loc)

Artillery along the Confederate line at Henry House Hill anchored and protected the infantry. (skb)

The ruins of the Henry House were photographed some months after the battle on July 21, 1861. Tragically, a widow—Judith Henry—was killed here in her home when an artillery shell crashed into her room during the first battle of Manassas. (loc)

Pelham took the battery to the vicinity of the Robinson House. This residence was owned by a wealthy, free African-American man, James Robinson. Today, just the outline of the house's foundation remains. (skb)

Alburtis's Battery headed to the front. "The battery under Lieutenant Pelham, came into action on the same line as the others; and nobly did the artillery maintain its position for hours against the enemy's advancing thousands." Second Lieutenant William T. Poague from the Rockbridge artillery recalled, "I was riding at the rear of the battery in column and behind me came Alburtis' guns in charge of a young officer. Just as we reached the top of the ridge next to Bull Run, he exclaimed, "I'll be dogged if I'm going any further back," and wheeled his guns into battery."

The topography on the right flank of the Confederate artillery line on Henry House Hill has several rises and low places that made good artillery advantage points around the Robinson House. According to account, Pelham moved his cannon multiple times during the battle, taking in this area.

Several rises and low places exist at that end of the artillery line around the Robinson House that were good artillery advantage points. Without the obstruction of battle smoke, a clear view extends from Pelham's position toward Henry House itself, the advanced location of Rickett's battery, and the open ground where Union troops tried to advance. Pelham also could have shifted west of the Robinson House location.

At least once, Pelham moved the battery to confront "a Federal brigade . . . lurking along under cover of the ridges and wood" and trying to flank the Confederate line. General Beauregard reported that the enemy's movement "was easily republished by Latham's battery . . . aided by Alburtis's Battery, opportunely sent to Latham's left by General Jackson, and supported by fragments of troops. . . ."

Colonel Burnside's Union soldiers rush forward during the battle of Manassas. In this woodcut image, the unit carries their flags—similar to the ones Pelham targeted and claimed he shot down during the fight. (loc)

Lt. Pelham's first experience under fire was intense. He later claimed "I was under a heavy fire of musketry and cannon for about seven hours, how I escaped or why I was spared a just God only knows." He wrote about bursting shell fragments raining down on his battery, a horse shot from under him, aiming guns, particularly shooting down three U.S. flags, and discovering that his men "were cool and brave and made terrible havoc on the enemy."

After intense fighting and close-range artillery duels on the plateau of Henry House Hill, the infantry of the 1st Virginia Brigade started a charge that pushed Union volunteers into a hurried and panicky retreat. Unleashed from Bald Hill, Confederate cavalry led by Col. James E. B. Stuart helped to capture prisoners and further hasten the Union troops' flight toward Washington D.C.

Pelham noted that "the victory was splendid and complete" and that he hoped "to write . . . from Washington City before many weeks." He was also thrilled with the captured artillery and ammunition, noting that among the taken guns he had recognized "the West Point battery that I have drilled with so often."

This photo comes from Gettysburg, but it represents the sort of tragedy strewn across the battlefield at Manassas. The sight of dead friends or strangers affected nearly all the participants and eyewitnesses of the battle. Pelham was no exception. (loc)

The Confederate battlefield victory along the banks of Bull Run and the rolling terrain of Manassas seemed to justify the Southerners' hopes for separation and independence, but their success had not been decisive enough to produce their desired political outcome. Instead, the defeated Union troops and home front increased their efforts to gather an army for an extended war—something beyond 90 days. The battle left soldiers on both sides reeling from the reality of war, even as they clung harder to their causes.

Like many other young officers at that first battle, Pelham faced a reckoning. In a letter to his father that was published in the local newspaper back in Alabama, the lieutenant offered his confession and justification:

Confederate General Thomas J. Jackson received the nickname "Stonewall" at this battle for refusing to leave his anchoring position on Henry House Hill. Today, a superhero-esque statue of Jackson overlooks the fields. (loc)

I have seen what Romancers call glorious war. I have seen it in all its phases. I have heard the booming of cannon, and the more deadly rattle of musketry at a distance—I have heard it all near by and have been under its destructive showers. I have seen men and horses fall thick and flat around me. I have seen our own men bloody and frightened flying before the enemy. I have seen them bravely charge the enemy's lines and heard the shout of triumph as they carried the position, I have heard the agonizing shrieks of the wounded and dying—I have passed over the battle field and seen the mangled forms of men and horses in frightful abundance. Men without heads, without arms, and others without legs. All this I have witnessed and more, till my heart

sickens; and war is not glorious as novelists would have us believe. It is only when we are in the heat and flush of battle that it is fascinating and interesting. It is only then that we enjoy it. When we forget ourselves and revel in the destruction we are dealing around us. I am now ashamed of the feelings I had in those hours of danger. The whistling bullets and shells were music to me, I gloried in it—it delighted and fascinated me—I feared not death in any forms; but when the battle was won and I visited the field a change came over me, I see the horrors of war, but it was necessary.

We are battling for our rights and homes. Ours is a just war, a holy cause. The invader must meet the fate he deserves and we must meet him as becomes us, as becomes men.

Pelham had accepted, supported, and was willing to die for the Confederate cause. His ideals of war had been shattered, but his beliefs in fearless manhood remained. He would stay and pursue the music of shells. He would live a story filled with glory and the horrors of war.

With Stonewall's statue and an artillery piece in this photographic shot, it's a foretelling of the military partnership Pelham and Jackson would forge and unleash at Manassas again nearly 13 months later. (skb)

Stuart Horse Artillery:
"Pelham is in command"

CHAPTER SIX

With caissons containing ammunition in the rear and cannons to the front, the Stuart Horse Artillery spent many hours drilling to be able to connect the horses, caissons, and cannons and move rapidly from position to position. (skb)

"It affords me indescribable pleasure to learn from your letter that you had discharged your duty in such a manner. . . . I know from Col. Martin's letter that you have done more and done better than your modesty permitted you to describe. If I have ever show you any friendship or favor I am amply compensated by the knowledge that you have act so nobly, so bravely and so skilfully[sp]," wrote Judge A. J. Walker in Alabama to Lt. Pelham ten days after the first battle of Manassas. The Confederate victory set the stage for longer war, and young officers looked to the future, preparing for more combat and seeking promotions. The Judge recognized this, advising Pelham that the victory would "exacerbate the enmity of the northern people and stimulate them to still greater exertions for our subjugation. You will yet have other opportunities to serve your county, and win for yourself renown. I know you will discharge your duty on every occasion. . . ." For Pelham, the means to his next opportunity lay in his artillery skill and in the plans of Gen. Stuart.

General James Ewell Brown "Jeb" Stuart envisioned batteries of horse artillery as part of the Confederate cavalry under his command that would increase the firepower and offensive and defensive opportunities to strike at opponents. (loc)

This illustration shows the horse team, the caisson, and the cannon all connected and galloping or bouncing along. While it was ideal to use roads, the horse artillery often rode over rough terrain to place the guns in more advantageous positions. (loc)

In the aftermath of Manassas, Pelham pulled several captured cannon into Alburtis's Battery and spent his days continuing to organize, supply, and further train that unit.   September came with a transfer. Pelham was ordered to take charge of Capt. Grove's Culpeper Battery. He found the battery in poor condition, with more than half the enlisted men deserted and more on sick leave. Pelham went to work to recruit for the battery and later secured ammunition and equipment from the Confederate War Department. His hard work and leadership skills did not pass unnoticed.

James Ewell Brown "Jeb" Stuart had commanded regiments of Confederate cavalry around Harpers Ferry and at First Manassas. On September 24, Stuart received a promotion to brigadier general and the authorization to reorganize cavalry for more effective service. A West Pointer graduate (Class of 1854), Stuart had spent a few years on the western frontier, helped capture abolitionist John Brown, and then resigned his commission to follow his home state of Virginia into the Confederacy. Stuart's aptitude for cavalry organization and tactics came with additional charisma flair and his determination to assume the role of a rollicking cavalier. Underneath Stuart's foppery and antics lay a talent for finding leaders and using cavalry to support, screen, and protect the infantry army.

Part of Stuart's vision for his cavalry included the concept of horse artillery. This type of unit had been developed on European battlefields and refined in Napoleon's tactics nearly half a century earlier. While equestrians pulled most of the field artillery on Civil War battlefields, horse artillery differed from other

cannon units. Horse artillery moved with the cavalry, and its artillerymen were mounted. The concept and tactics called for rapid movement, deployment, firing, and relocation—mobile firepower. Working with cavalry to harass, delay, and protect, well-trained horse artillery could deliver a punch to the enemy, then gallop away to another position. On November 11, 1862, the Confederate secretary of war authorized the formation of the Stuart Horse Artillery.

Stuart's preferences for a commander—John E. Cooke, a relative of Stuart's wife, and James W. Breathed—did not meet approval from authorities in Richmond. Additionally, Cooke showed little enthusiasm for the opportunity, preferring to spend his time in the Confederate capital. Breathed would be involved with the horse artillery and one of the commanders after Pelham when his name was better recognized. Pelham showed an active interest in the horse artillery from an early stage of its formation. Stuart wrote to his wife on November 24, 1861, that "John Pelham wants it and he may get it. . . . I need a commander very much to organize the battery forthwith."

By December 4, Stuart announced to his wife that "the Horse Artillery is growing rapidly . . . Pelham is in command of it and there are three acting Lieutenants—Fauntleroy, Breathed, and Brown."

While horses or mules moved most field cannons during the Civil War, "Horse Artillery" differed since the cannoneers were mounted too—allowing gunners and cannons to move rapidly and keep up with the cavalry. Note the mounted artillerymen in this 1862 image of Union Horse Artillery. (loc)

A week later the general wrote that the battery was "under the energetic management of Pelham" and "will tell a tale in the battle. It has taken the name of 'Stuart Horse Artillery.'"

Pelham did the unglamorous work of building and training this battery. Some of his paperwork survives, showing his efforts to find horses, forage, supplies, ammunition, and gunners. Even the practical supplies of "20 skillets and 20 Camp Kettles" had to be obtained. Present and available for duty, Pelham won the appointment and the appreciation of the recruited men.

During the winter months, Pelham may have returned to Alabama or had someone else leading recruiting efforts in his home county. An appealing article with lavish language appeared in the Jacksonville Republican newspaper. "Capt. John Pelham, of Calhoun county . . . is authorized to raise two hundred volunteers for mounted Artillerists, to serve during the war. The Confederate States will furnish 240 horses, and eight splendid brass cannon, wagons, caissons and equipments complete for men and horse." He explained that his unit "has the novelty of being the only one in our service—in fact the only one in America." Pelham promised "the service will be active and energetic. . . . The career of this company is destined to be a brilliant one; and whenever or where ever there is likely to be a fight, they are bound to be in the front. . . ."

The third-person notice may have been written by Pelham or by an editor, family member, or other recruiting officer. At the end of the article, an "extract from a private letter," purporting to be written by Pelham including a recognition of women's power on the home front in recruiting efforts. "Now is the time to serve your county—enlist the interest of the Ladies—tell them I want to do something to render myself worthy of them, and they must aid in furnishing men. I have got the finest equipment and the finest guns in the service, and I want good men to man them."

Whether Pelham journeyed south or stayed in Virginia organizing his new recruits, his influence and connections need to be understood. The Pelham family held prominence in their county, and from West Point letters and other fragments of correspondence, John Pelham had the interest of Confederate Alabama politicians at local, state, and national levels. His position as an Alabama cadet at West Point had increased his importance, and political influencers watched his military career and successes. Pelham likely used these connections to his advantage as he formed the Stuart Horse Artillery. His recruiting earned him a $600 bounty reward for signing up so many volunteers.

Records for the Stuart Horse Artillery are fragmentary, but surviving pieces point to the far-reaching recruiting efforts that Pelham used as he strove to build an elite and privileged unit. At least 40 men from Alabama joined, and there was a legendary contingency of gunners hailing from New Orleans which became known as the "Napoleon Detachment," inspired by their French-Creole heritage and their 12-pound Napoleon cannon. Pelham enlisted Virginians from the area of his encampment. One gunner claimed, "Our Battery was very cosmopolitan in its make up. We enrolled men from Maryland, Virginia, South Carolina, Georgia, Alabama, Mississippi, Louisiana, and Tennessee."

Enlistment advertisements promised the benefits of an elite unit with the government providing the horses, but to fulfill the goal of being "in the front" at a battle, the new gunners had to learn their duties. Pelham's drillmaster skills kept his recruits at work through the chilly winter months as they worked to master the steps to fire a cannon and learn to control their artillery in all types of terrain and tactical

Presumably a war-era sketch of John Pelham and likely from late 1862 or 1863 since there is a single-star insignia on his collar that would be consistent with the rank of major. (jpha)

scenarios. Regarding the young lieutenant's control of his men, gunner and color-bearer Robert L. Mackall claimed Pelham "didn't say much. He didn't need to. He would look at you and you felt his eyes going through you and all of a sudden you felt pretty mean. I saw the fellows stammer and blush before him; the biggest and the strongest just wilted when he called them to account. . . . It wasn't good to fool with orders around John Pelham!"

Learning the practicalities of camp life and artillery horsemanship was one of the first challenges for the Stuart Horse Artillerymen. As they arrived, they settled into camp at near Stuart's cavalry headquarters at Camp "Qui Vive" for the winter months. Besides military training and duties, horse artillerymen had extra tasks to look after the dozens of horses assigned to their battery. Some gunners brought enslaved men to with them to do camp chores, look after the picket lines of horses, and perform skilled tasks like horseshoeing.

On the drill ground, Pelham and his officers taught about deadly tactics and how to load and fire their cannons. Initially, 18 men were assigned to each cannon in the Stuart Horse Artillery. (This number fluctuated widely during the campaign months as casualties and reorganizing took their toll.) It did not take 18 men to fire a cannon, but additional riders and gunners managed the teams of horses and the ammunition. Everything needed to deliver that rapid firepower had to roll with the cannon and caisson and always be mobile.

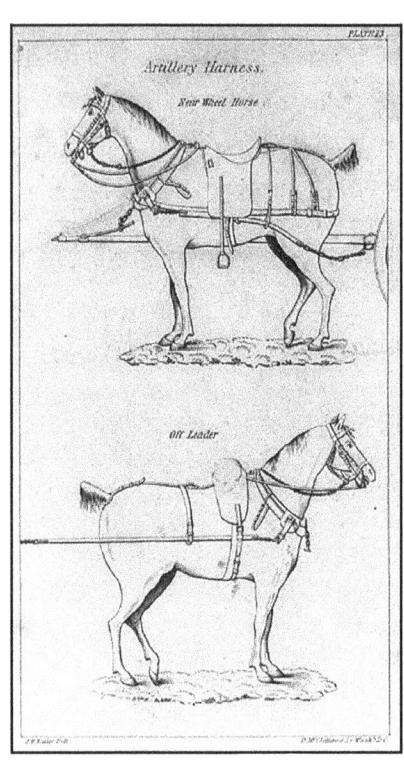

An illustration from an artillery manual showing the harness of a horse. Pelham's years of farm work likely gave him experience for placing horses in the teams based on their pulling capabilities. (loc)

Throughout its field action, the Stuart Horse Artillery used a variety of cannons. Spring 1862 found the unit with two 6 lb. Howitzers, two 12 lb. Howitzers, one Napoleon, and one 3-inch Blakely rifle, and presumably they had drilled with these (or some of these) cannons during the winter. Pelham or his lieutenants selected the cannons for specific jobs and ranges in combat.

A limber—two-wheeled conveyance—carried an ammunition chest and the team of 6 horses were

This photograph of Union artillery men shows an ideal number of men to fire the cannon. Note the sponge or ramrod that one artilleryman is holding, and a man to the right of the cannon's muzzle is holding a shell. (loc)

hitched to its front. Buckets and other equipment to protect the ammunition from weather was stowed in or on the limber. The cannon could be attached to the limber, but a caisson with more ammunition chests could be placed between the limber and the gun, too.

A caisson typically carried two ammunition chests and was hooked behind the limber with a long. Hauling a caisson with the limber gave the advantage of more ammunition that could replenish the limber's ammunition chest. The caisson often included a spare wheel and other helpful equipment. The cannon could be attached to the back of the caisson, making a compact connection and moveable set: horses, limber, caisson, cannon.

The contents of an ammunition chest varied, depending on the type of cannon it would serve. Different types of cannons took different ammunition sizes. However, the basic ammunition used in combat remained similar: solid shot, shell, grapeshot, and cannister. The battery commander ordered different types of ammunition based on the range and purpose. Cannister and grapeshot blasted metal balls "shotgun

The Stuart Horse Artillery formed in late 1861, and Pelham became their first commander. In the following war years, the unit expanded and continued to operate after Pelham's death. This image shows some marker cannons and a plaque for the Stuart Horse Artillery at East Cavalry Field at Gettysburg National Military Park. (skb)

Pelham did not like to leave a strategic position until all the ammunition in the caisson had been fired. (skb)

style" into advancing infantry or cavalry, typically at close range. Shells—and there were many types— exploded mid-air and rained metal fragments onto an enemy's position; a fuse in the shell had to be prepared and literally cut to a specific length to explode at the right time to hit the targets. Solid shot ploughed through an enemy's formation or dueled with other artillery.

To fire the cannon, the gunners unfastened it from the limber and caisson and maneuvered it by hand into position. The assigned gun crew knew their roles, and the steps to prepare, load, and fire the cannon were like field artillery. The differences came with limbering and moving the cannon between shots to stay close to the enemy or reposition as a defensive tactic.

At full strength, nine men handled firing the cannon. The men occupied numbered positions based on their tasks when firing. The "Chief of the Piece"– usually a Gun Corporal or Gun Sergeant–called the orders to his crew and received orders from the Gun Officer. When the order "Load" resounded, #1 moved to the muzzle of the cannon, holding a rammer at the ready. #8 observed at the limber or ammunition chest, serving as "Chief of the Caisson", and coordinating with Gun Corporal and the battery commander. #6 and #7 at the ammunition chest handed the ammunition to #5 after selecting the correct type of projectile and cut fuses to the correct distance, if needed. #5 rushed the ammunition in a leather bag to #2 who placed it in the

muzzle; then #1 rammed the projectile to the back of the cannon. Meanwhile, #3 covered the cannon's vent hole with his thumb, protected by a leather thumbstall, to prevent sparking as the gunpowder and shot were rammed. Next, the gunner sergeant sighted the piece and followed directives from the battery's officer, who was either mounted or on foot observing the target and judging the precise direction and elevation needed to hit the target. Now the cannoneers waited for the command "Ready" to start their next steps. #3 inserted a vent pick into the cannon's vent hole and pierced into the charge of gunpowder. #4 then placed a lanyard to a friction primer and slipped the primer into the vent. "Fire" called the gunner sergeant or the battery officer, and #4 pulled the lanyard while the other men leaned away from the cannon, and all positioned to avoid the coming recoil. If the cannon was ordered to fire again at this place, the cannoneers rolled the piece back to position or man-handled it to a slightly different position. #1 ran a wet sponge down the barrel of the cannon to ensure that no sparks or embers remained. Then the process began again. A well-drilled gun crew could fire two or three shots per minute.

This process had to be precise to ensure the maximum safety (of operations) for the gun crew and the most effective firing. However, the crew needed to know how to perform all the positions since in combat or the frequent times of under strength, cannoneers needed to step into a vacancy or perform

A sight at the end of this cannon is a reminder of the science of artillery. A battery commander called degrees of elevation and points of direction to direct the shots toward a target and usually watched the results of the firing through field glasses, calling adjustments as needed. (skb)

multiple tasks to keep the cannon firing. At times, Pelham—though battery commander—dismounted and worked on the gun crew, setting an example of knowledge and leadership.

Meanwhile, another set of cannoneers managed the team of horses. Typically, six horses pulled each cannon during the march or on the battlefield. Unlike

field artillery, which sent their horse teams further to the rear, the horse artillery kept their means of swift transportation close. They would hitch the cannon to the limber after one or two shots and change position, unhook the cannon, and start firing again. Maneuvering the horses and keeping them calm may not have seemed as glamorous as working the cannon, but it was a crucial part of the success of a horse artillery gun. The speed and responsiveness of the horses ensured that the cannon could be placed and unlimbered within seconds.

Venting holes and placement for the fuse and lanyard are located on the top rear of a cannon's barrel on most Civil War era guns. (skb)

The training Pelham put his cannoneers through during the winter of 1861-1862 forged his battery into a fighting force that would be adaptable and able to develop their skills in the coming campaigns. Speed and dash characterized the movements and fire patterns, and to accomplish their battlefield objectives, they had to know their places and perform their duties with precision. Pelham and the battery's lieutenants chose the cannons' placements and called the range and coordinates for precise shots.

Pelham himself falls silent in surviving primary sources for this winter. Some military paperwork and supply requests exist. Years later, another officer offered criticism that Pelham did not maintain order in his battery and that he used horses irresponsibly. The nature of horse artillery lends itself to expendable horses in the need for swiftness, something not readily understood by other field artillerists. In organization, Pelham may have failed to keep written records for the unit (or they may have been lost or destroyed), but battlefield results pointed to a level of cohesion and organization that existed beyond or without bureaucratic forms.

What others witnessed on the battlefields came through hours of practice and preparation. Pvt. David Cardwell later described the Stuart Horse Artillery in action, and the quote can be seen as the proof of Pelham's winter work:

The guns rush for the hills behind us, six horses to a piece, three riders to each gun, over dry ditches where a farmer would not drive a wagon, through clumps of bushes, over logs a foot thick, every horse on a gallop, every rider lashing his team and yelling. . . . The guns jump two feet high as the heavy wheels strike rock or log, but not a horse slackens his pace, the cannoneer leaning forward in his saddle. Six guns, six caissons, six horses each, eighty men race for the brow of the hill. . . . A moment ago the battery was a confused mob; we look again, and the six guns are in position, the detached horses hurrying away, the ammunition chests open. . . . 'Boom, boom!' opens the battery, and jets of fire jump down to scorch the green trees. . . . What grim, cool fellows those cannoneers are! Every man is a perfect machine. Bullets splash dust in their faces, but they do not wince; bullets sing over and around them, but they do not dodge. There goes one to the earth, shot through the head as he sponged the gun. The machinery loses just one beat, misses just one cog in the wheel, and then works away again as before. Every gun is using short-fuse shells. The ground shakes and trembles.

As 1861 rolled to 1862, that vision of battlefield combat for the Stuart Horse Artillery still lingered in the distance, but it would be their destiny through the training that Pelham put the horses, men, and guns through. In the coming year of battles, Pelham had to prove the success of his leadership and provide the swift, mobile firepower that Stuart wanted to explode chaos and death on unsuspecting enemies.

On the Peninsula:
"They fear Stuart's battery"

CHAPTER SEVEN

The Stuart Horse Artillery rolled down the main street of Williamsburg toward their first combat experience in May 1862. They passed Bruton Parish Church where one of John Pelham's ancestor's had played the church organ during the Colonial Era. (skb)

The dogwoods and red buds bloomed in spring 1862 as military events pressured the Confederacy and Virginia. In the West, Forts Henry and Donelson had surrendered to Union Gen. Ulysses S. Grant, opening the gateway to Tennessee, and a desperate two-day battle at Shiloh ended in a Confederate defeat. The Virginian Shenandoah Valley saw Union invasion, and "Stonewall" Jackson suffered a defeat and long retreat before striking back and winning five battles in his famed Valley Campaign. Union Gen. George B. McClellan transported his more than 100,000-man Army of the Potomac by water from Washington City to the Virginia Peninsula, intending to march nearly 80 miles and capture Richmond, the Confederate capital. To meet this threat, Gen. Johnston shifted most of his army from northern and central Virginia to the Peninsula or around Richmond. The besieged Confederacy looked for leaders to save them and that they could hero-worship. General Stuart, his cavalry, and his horse artillery were willing to aim a shot in the quest for glory.

Pelham had enlisted enough cannoneers into the Stuart Horse Artillery that the battery was officially mustered on March 23, 1862. Four lieutenants—James Breathed, William McGregor, William Elston, and James Shephard—took their places and commissions. The noncommissioned officers were assigned. John Pelham received the votes to be the battery's Captain. The Virginian governor approved the commission on May 1, appointing Pelham as an officer in the Provisional Army of Virginia, officially claiming the Stuart Horse Artillery as a Virginia unit despite its state-diverse recruiting.

By April 9, 1862, Pelham's battery rolled south, toward the Peninsula to join the defense. Records show that at the beginning of the Peninsula Campaign, this single battery of horse artillery contained 141 men and had 8 cannon. The concept of horse artillery would be tested as Stuart transformed his cavalry from pickets to a force to scout quickly and launch various surprises against Union forces. Horse artillery added to the firepower that the Confederate cavalry used to deliver an offensive punch or defensively cover their raids.

A signed Carte-de-Visite of John Pelham, copied from his West Point uniform photograph. (loc)

Pelham's first campaign in 1862 hit a rocky start on the march. The weather poured rain, snow, and sleet, turning the roads to mud and forcing the cavalry and horse artillery to abandon their baggage wagons with their tents and personal supplies. At some point in Henrico County, near Richmond, Pelham confiscated two mules and a harness from a civilian, giving a certificate for the beasts but not the leathers. The civilian got angry, and a chain of letters passed between Richmond officers and Gen. Stuart about the incident. Stuart defended Pelham and eventually the incident passed. While the requisitioned mules seemed important to the outraged civilian, more pressing matters unfolded at the eastern end of the Virginian Peninsula.

With other elements of Johnston's army, Stuart and Pelham arrived near the Confederate lines at Yorktown around April 21, 1862, joining Gen. Magruder's approximately 10,000 Confederates, vastly outnumbered by McClellan's Army of the Potomac ponderously advancing along the Peninsula. The artillery headed for Bigler's Wharf on the James River, joining forces with other Confederate artillery commanded to guard against Union landings. However, on May 3, Gen. Joseph E. Johnston ordered the Confederates to evacuate Yorktown and head northwest up the Peninsula. Stuart's cavalry acted as rearguard as the army pulled back. Near Williamsburg—the old colonial-era capital of Virginia—two Union divisions plunged toward the rear of the Confederate army but met resistance near Fort Magruder, overlooking the intersection of Lee's Mill Road and Yorktown Road and about one mile from the town of Williamsburg. Confederate Gen. James Longstreet put his infantry division in a defensive position, and the battle of Williamsburg unfolded on May 5, 1862.

General George B. McClellan brought the Union Army of the Potomac to the Virginia Peninsula in the spring of 1862, intending to march on Richmond—the capital of the Confederacy. (loc)

Stuart ordered Pelham to the battlefield, and after struggling over muddy roads, he arrived around 2:00 p.m. with "two 12-pounder howitzers and one 12-pound rifled gun, Blakely." Moving "to the right and in front of Fort Magruder," Pelham "opened fire on the enemy" and "held this position under a heavy fire until General [D. H.] Hill's brigade moved up and deployed in front of my battery, when I moved to the left and took position on the Yorktown Road, to enfilade the enemy's line." He struggled as the Blakely gun's elevating screw collapsed, but managed to temporarily repair the gun, staying "until 5 P.M., when I withdrew for want of ammunition." Pelham detailed in his report that his guns had fired 360 rounds of ammunition during the battle and praised his officers and cannoneers for their "commendable calmness and courage." The butcher's bill for Pelham's gunners was two wounded men, four dead horses, three wounded horses, and 13 escaped animals, though most were eventually retrieved.

The Stuart Horse Artillery's baptism of fire at Williamsburg had proven their value. They had held position until infantry could form a line and then moved to the enemy's flank to deliver deadly artillery fire. Artillerist George Shreve later remembered the reactions of the men under fire at Williamsburg: "Some men who were very timid at first, afterward, made good soldiers. I have in mind, a boy about nineteen who was in the first battle . . . in serving the gun, ran away some fifty feet or more, from the gun, and could hardly be persuaded to return, being so frightened. Sgt. Chichester went after him, and placing himself behind him, with both hands on his shoulders, forced him forward to his post, and threatened to shoot him if he deserted again. He made a good soldier, and never showed cowardice after that." Stuart only had praise for Pelham and the horse artillery.

Stuart's first ride around McClellan occurred in June 1862. Though some cannons from the Stuart Horse Artillery made the ride, Pelham did not go—perhaps due to illness or camp-based duties. (loc)

The battle of Williamsburg ended inconclusively. The Confederates continued to retreat, and the Union army slowly pursued. Again, Pelham and his guns stayed in the rear of the army, occasionally taking the opportunity to fire at Col. William W. Averell's Union cavalry as the retreat continued toward New Kent Court House. Private Walters explained to his wife, "They fear Stuart's battery. They say they don't like to be fired on by cannons from every old field. . . ." At several bridges over the Chickahominy River, Pelham engaged Union forces. Stuart wrote on May 17, "Just as I expected for . . . as I arrived at this point the enemy's advance was announced, and after . . . crossing the Chickahominy before them, burnt the bridge, and gave them a slap in the face with Pelham's battery which sent them howling back in confusion."

As McClellan sought a way to cross the Chickahominy's swampy, stagnant water, the infantry battle of Seven Pines broke out on May 31. Confederate Gen. Johnston was wounded in this battle, and Gen. Robert E. Lee arrived to take command of the army, which reformed on the outskirts of their capital city. McClellan stalled, begging for more troops. Lee ordered entrenchments to be dug and then forged a daring plan for Stuart's cavalry. A ride around McClellan's army could reveal potential weaknesses and confirm the precision locations of the Union army's flanks. Stuart selected 1,200 cavalrymen for this ride that would total nearly 150 miles. Two guns from the Stuart Horse Artillery, commanded by Lt. James Breathed and Lt. William McGregor joined the force.

Pelham missed the expedition and was not mentioned in reports about the Ride Around McClellan; instead, Stuart took battery lieutenants instead of the horse artillery's captain. It is unlikely that Pelham had offended Stuart, opening the question about his absence. Contextually, it is most likely that Pelham either had command duties that absolutely prevented his absence from the remaining battery, or he was ill. Debilitating illnesses tore through the ranks of both armies around the Chickahominy. Malarial fevers, typhoid, and dysentery confined soldiers and officers to their tents or forced them to hospitals. Even though Pelham did not participate in this ride around McClellan, it had far-reaching effects for his guns. Nineteenth-century artillery historian J. C. Wise noted: "Perhaps nothing that occurred during the early days of

Preserved earthworks of Fort Magruder remain on the outskirts of historic Williamsburg. Pelham's first battle leading the Stuart Horse Artillery took place near this fort. (skb)

A crossroads outside of Fort Magruder and Pelham's approximate position for part of the battle of Williamsburg. (skb)

"Stonewall" Jackson particularly noted Pelham's artillery skill during the battle of Gaines's Mill and met the young artillerist. An artillerist during the Mexican-American War, Jackson admired bold artillery tactics and came to trust Pelham's judgment. (loc)

the war so awakened the Army to the possibilities of the more mobile guns as did this raid around McClellan, in which Pelham['s guns] took part."

Three days after their departure on June 12, Stuart and his horsemen returned with captured prisoners and horses, losing one killed, a few wounded, and one prisoner. The information Stuart had obtained revealed that the Union's right was completely vulnerable, and Lee began to act upon the details, even as Richmonders' celebrated Stuart's ride.

"Stonewall" Jackson had temporarily halted the Union's ventures in the Shenandoah Valley and now brought his divisions to join Lee's new, active defense of Richmond. Lee tasked Stuart with working with Jackson as he headed for the exposed flank of the Union army. Pelham and his guns helped to secure a crucial bridge over Totopotomoy Creek on June 25, but Jackson's infantry moved sluggishly—exhausted from their Valley Campaign and semi-lost in unfamiliar territory. McClellan consolidated his army, pulling in the exposed flank after the battle of Mechanicsville on June 26, and drawing the Confederates toward a battle at Gaines's Mill.

Pelham continued with Jackson's troops as sounds of battle sounded on June 27. One of Stuart's staff officers remembered, "The infantry got well to work by two o'clock, and from that time the action was very severe. We were in reserve, but Stuart, with his usual enterprise, was riding everywhere, looking for chances to put in his cavalry, and with Pelham's guns he did some good service on the flanks of the enemy." Pelham cleared out some Union cavalry along Old Church Road with a few well-placed shots, opening the road for Jackson's slow advance.

In the late afternoon, Jackson finally arrived at Gaines's Mill, but his artillery lingered behind the infantry. Stuart ordered Pelham to go into action on the left flank of Jackson's forming line, near Old Cold Harbor Tavern. Rolling a Blakely rifle cannon and a 12-pound Napoleon into position, Pelham engaged two Union artillery batteries across the fields, commanded by Stephen Weed and John C. Tidball. Within minutes, Union fire had knocked the Blakely out of action, but with the lone Napoleon, Pelham held position and fought back against the batteries.

A choppy set of scribbles in John Esten Cooke's diary notes gives a glimpse of the confusion of the fight through the eyes of a staff officer:

> *Sent about with orders. Pelham with a gun sent forward into field to left of front of Cold Harbor. Opened hotly—batteries of the enemy replied. Shelling still hotter. Sent by Stuart to order up Cobb Legion—a squadron—to support Pelham. Cobb had changed his position, and gone into the woods to avoid the shells. Could find him nowhere. . . . Joined Stuart and Jackson near Tree Hd. Qrs. Pelham still fighting like a trump. Reported: Stuart, Jackson others & myself went forward toward Pelham—musketry terrible. Artillery duel in full roar. Shells hot and furious. Enemy's battery at last quieter.*

As Confederate troops came to battle near Gaines's Mill, confusion over roads and road names delayed the arrival of some units. Pelham's guns helped to hold the position around Old Cold Harbor Tavern (no longer standing) until more troops arrived. (skb)

William P. Walters of the horse artillery wrote with unique spelling that left "with one gun I ramed[sp] the balls down as fast as I cood we all worked hard captain pelham helped us himself." As the new Confederate cannons eventually arrived, "the captain told us to quit firing and rest rest does good eaven when it is taken under a shower of balls for for we soon commensed agane like fresh set of boys and soon heard the last Gun of our enemy groaning threw the are."

Looking over the "fields of fire" that Pelham's guns covered during the early hours of the battle of Gaines's Mill. (skb)

As the duel ended and the Confederate infantry surged forward to secure a victory that day, Pelham received a summons. He joined Stuart and was formally introduced to "Stonewall" Jackson. The terse general had a habit of spotting artillery talent and had a long-standing passion for cannon, going back to his days in the U.S. Mexico War. Jackson had noticed Pelham with Alburtis's Battery at Manassas, but now he had witnessed the effectiveness of the horse artillery. Able to move quicker than the field artillery, they had secured and fought for a position while the rest of Jackson's forces deployed. The longer-standing military partnership between Jackson and Stuart now included Pelham, and the action at Gaines's Mill forged a trust that would be put to the test on future battlefields.

Sometime later, Pelham walked on the battlefield. Whether he looked for a fallen comrade, tried to find meaning in the day's combat, or surveyed, the ground is unclear. Somewhere, he picked up an Episcopal Prayer Book. On the inside of the cover, he wrote "Picked up on the battlefield at Cold Harbor. J. P." Either sent by mail or gifted later in person, he eventually gave it to Sallie Dandridge, a young woman who lived near Martinsburg, Virginia (now West Virginia).

With no time to rest after the fight near Gaines's Mill, Stuart and the cavalry saddled and rode 15 miles

east to the Pamunkey River the following day. They aimed for White House Landing, a strongly guarded Union supply base. William Blackford recorded:

This portion of Hickory Neck Church was built in 1774, and it survived when the other parts of the church were destroyed in 1825. As Confederate troops retreated up the Peninsula after the battle of Williamsburg, Pelham camped with the Horse Artillery near this historic structure. (skb)

> *Not being able to take it, the next best thing was to make them destroy the vast depot of supplies at the place; and to this end Stuart dismounted some of his men and marched them about in sight of their lines to make them think we had infantry, and then he made Pelham fire quantities of ammunition at long range into the place, changing the position of the guns from time to time to make them think we had a great number. The ruse succeeded and soon after nightfall great columns of smoke and a bright illumination announced that they were setting fire to the great town of canvas and board houses that had sprung up at the place since its occupation by the Northern army.*

That same day, Pelham fought a Union gunboat for the first time. Galloping along the shore and using the foliage to hide his positions, the captain used a howitzer to force sharpshooters on the USS Marblehead's deck into hiding. Stuart reported, "The howitzer gave chase at a gallop, the more to cause the apprehension of being cut off below than of really effecting anything. The gunboat never returned."

After the Union abandoned the White House Landing, the Confederate cavalry lingered, finalizing the destruction and ensuring that McClellan did not retreat down the Peninsula in that direction Stuart ordered Pelham to put some well-placed shots through several train locomotives at the landing that could not be salvaged or moved. Then the cavalry turned to rejoin the main Confederate army which had continued pushing, fighting, and forcing the Union corps away from Richmond and south toward the James River.

Again, Pelham and his guns cleared the way for the cavalry column, notably at Forge Bridge on the Chickahominy River. As the Confederates occupied the former Federal position near Forge Bridge the day after Pelham's skirmish, one soldier saw "a dead horse, and under the cedars farther on two freshly made graves—silent witnesses of Pelham's death-dealing shots seen by us the day previous." On the Virginia Peninsula and during the Seven Days' Battles, Pelham trialed his tactics of clearing the way and holding positions and proved his deadly precision.

Before the cavalry rejoined Lee, the battle of Malvern Hill on July 1 had been fought and McClellan continued his retreat along the banks of the James River. The Union commander explained it was just a "change of bases," but his soldiers felt demoralized by the constant fighting and continual withdrawals. Rejoining the Confederate army at the end of the Seven Days' Battles, Stuart gave Pelham a chance to fire some parting shots.

Consulting with some local scouts, Pelham discovered that the Union army had left Evelynton Heights unguarded and sent a note, informing Stuart. The high ground overlooked the Union camp, which had its back to the James River. On the morning of July 3, Stuart ordered Pelham to open fire, instead of waiting for Confederate infantry to arrive as support. The rushed beginning turned semi-disastrous as the Union troops recovered from their panic and started fighting back. Without Confederate infantry backing, the cavalry and horse artillery were eventually forced to fall back.

The Peninsula Campaign and Seven Days' Battles had been a testing ground for Stuart's cavalry and Pelham's artillery. While not all went well or

according to plan, their successes were notable. Pelham's guns covered retreats, cleared roads, held positions until infantry or field artillery arrived, and took unconventional roles, like fighting gunboats. With McClellan's threat to Richmond neutralized, the Confederacy celebrated its summer saviors. Stuart had a growing list of exploits and many of his stories included his chief of artillery. The informal propaganda campaign was about to start, and more Union armies headed for the vulnerable railroads in Virginia, giving more opportunity to put horse artillery to use in the field and parlors.

This dirt road runs near White House Plantation on the Pamunkey River, reminiscent of the roads that the Stuart Horse Artillery traveled during their exploits in the Peninsula Campaign. (skb)

Second Manassas:

"To engage my battery where fitting opportunity should occur"

CHAPTER EIGHT

What was the use of having fine cavalry and horse artillery if no one knew about it? What was the point of being victorious and not celebrating? Life at Gen. Stuart's headquarters had military duties and mandatory social events. Technically, Pelham was not on Stuart's staff, but the general regularly insisted that Pelham live at the noisy headquarters. In July 1862, Stuart took advantage of his proximity to Richmond to create a social scene and military moment. Pelham found himself at the center of attention in Stuart's social court.

According to staff officer William Blackford, Pelham was "so innocent looking, so 'child-like and bland' in the expression of his sparkling blue eyes. . . . He was tall, slender, beautifully proportioned and very graceful, a superb rider, and brave as Julius Caesar." Blackford also claimed that Pelham was "the grandest flirt that ever lived." Exactly what Blackford meant by that sentiment, written after Pelham's death, is not quite clear (see Appendix A). Others in Pelham's peer group remarked more consistently on his humility that

During the battle of Second Manassas, Pelham had permission to place his cannons anywhere advantageous—a remarkable allowance from Gen. Jackson.
(skb)

General Robert E. Lee had driven McClellan from the gates of Richmond during the Seven Days Battles, then sent his two corps northward to confront Union Gen. John Pope. The battles of Cedar Mountain and Second Manassas were the result. (loc)

sometimes came across as bashful. "He never spoke of himself; you might live with him for a month, and never know that he had been in a single action. He never seemed to think that he deserved any applause for his splendid courage, and was silent upon all subjects connected with his own actions." It was easy to get "confuse him, and make him blush," making Pelham an easy target for Stuart's stories and regular teasing.

Pelham had social skills and, from his West Point letters, did not seem to be socially uncomfortable in parlors or on the dance floor. However, a few hints written by fellow officers suggest Pelham may not have been entirely comfortable with Stuart's teasing and matchmaking efforts. Depending on Pelham's personality, the wild hilarity at Stuart's headquarters may have worn on him. Around Stuart, practical jokes were endless, teasing continued long-term, and several musicians lived at headquarters to play whenever the general ordered entertainment or dancing. Stuart thrived on distractionism, and it may have been part of his strategy to prevent dwelling on the realities of war. One officer noted that the more outgoing Stuart was, the more likely there would be a dangerous raid or operation.

Drawing hints about Pelham's personality from his West Point letters, he seemed to enjoy parties and social interactions in moderation. Did his habits and temperament change during the war to be more outgoing or become more focused and possibly semi-withdrawn? His letter after First Manassas suggests an internal struggle with his feelings in combat and the reality of his battlefield exploits. Combat animated and enthused him like nothing else, but the weight of his successful killing seemed to burden and possibly guilt him. Artillery command required the intensity of finding a target and deciding on the trajectory of the ammunition to hit the target. Pelham observed— and sometimes up-close with field glasses—the effects of his shots. He saw ranks of men torn apart, horses eviscerated, enemy caissons or cannons exploding. Pelham was good at killing, and he knew it. His discomfort in talking about his battlefield actions or hearing Stuart retell the stories may have stemmed from a consciousness of doing his duty well, but also knowing that his success came with death and destruction. Unfortunately, with the loss of Pelham's letters, his thoughts and views are missing from this period of his life.

Pelham had not been militarily idle during the social weeks. Surviving paperwork shows that he had ordered forage for 180 horses and more cooking utensils for his men. Recruits continued joining the horse artillery, and he had to inspect and manage the new cannons and other equipment that he received from the captured bounty from the Peninsula.

In early August, Stuart's cavalry and Pelham's artillery rode north and forced a Union expedition to return to Fredericksburg, preventing their destruction of the Richmond, Fredericksburg & Potomac Railroad. The use of cavalry forces to temporarily halt or stall Union movements played out across Central Virginia. By August 15, one artilleryman wrote to his wife: "we have been all over eastern Virginia and in 33 skirmishes and 2 regular fights." Stuart and Pelham took their troopers to confront and harass Union Gen. John Pope's army as he operated in Culpeper County and then started retreating north. Working in unison with Gen. Jackson, the Confederate cavalry hovered around Pope, troubling to the Federals, especially along the rivers' fords. On August 22, Pelham took four guns to Freeman's Ford on the Rappahannock River and fired at Union Gen. Robert Milroy's infantry and a Union battery. The long-range duel lasted two hours, but Pelham "tried in vain to silence the enemy guns." Other artillery joined the fight and the Confederate infantry moved ahead, covered by the cannons, and Confederate cavalry prepared for a raid on Pope's headquarters.

Stuart continued to pursue and harass Union troops, and Pelham joined the Confederate infantry at Manassas Junction. Here, Jackson's men had captured supplies and weapons, and Pelham took the captured cannons, adding to 3-inch ordinance rifles to his battery's collection and trading out two of the 12-pound howitzers. Stuart later noted: "Captain Pelham, arriving late, was indefatigable in his efforts to

Union General John Pope commanded the Army of Virginia. His experiments with elements of total war against the civilian population enraged Confederate troops. (loc)

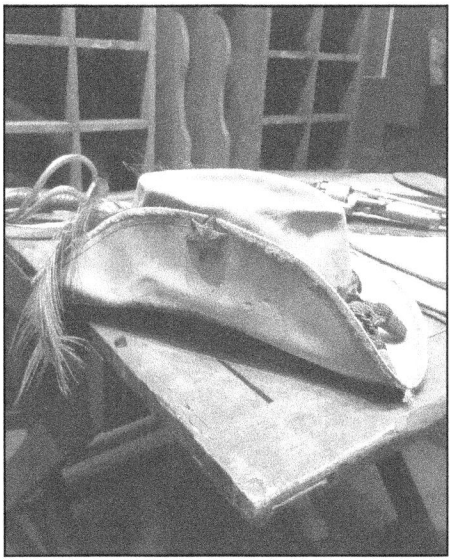

Jeb Stuart's famous feathered hat is now preserved and displayed at the American Civil War Museum in Richmond. However, it was captured during the summer of 1862 and eventually traded back, exchanged for Pope's cape. (skb)

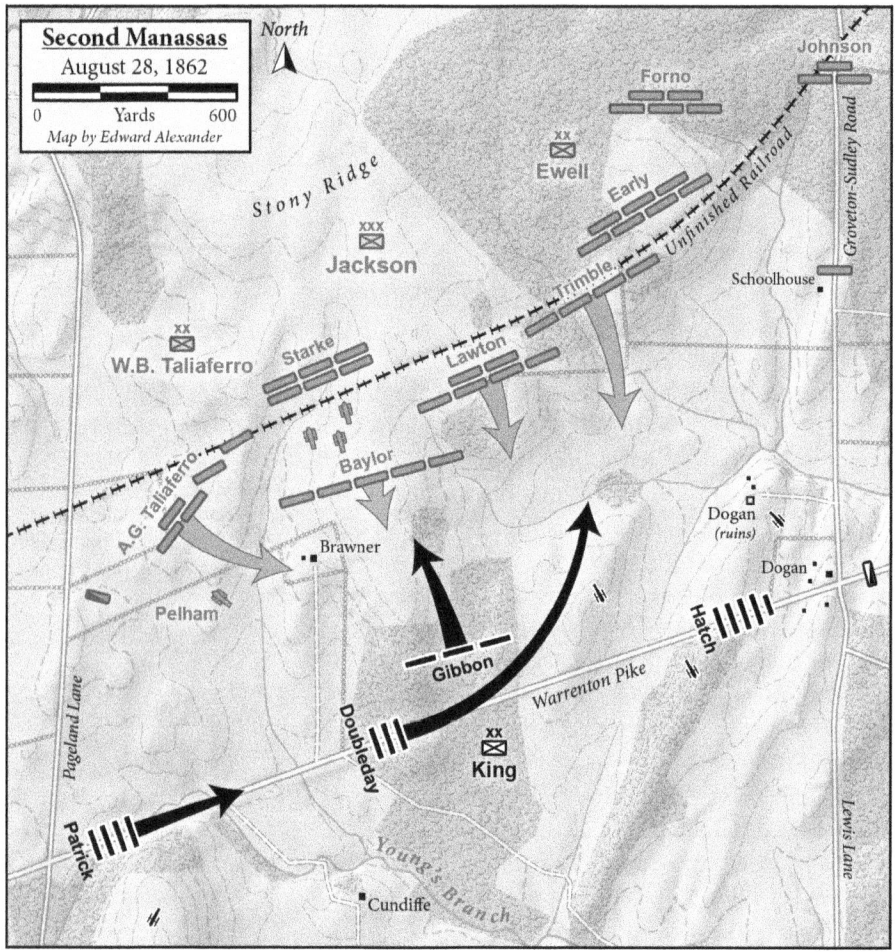

Second Manassas
August 28, 1862

0   Yards   600
Map by Edward Alexander

North

SECOND MANASSAS—During the battle of Second Manassas, Pelham fired artillery shots at Union infantry as they passed on the Warrenton Pike.

get away the captured guns, which duty was intrusted specially to him."

On August 28, Pelham left Centreville, covering the rear of Jackson's infantry. Near Lewis Ford on Bull Run, Union cavalry threatened, and Pelham ordered Lt. Breathed to drive off the riders with "a few well-directed shots." Skirting around the slower moving infantry on the Warrenton Pike, Pelham and his battery passed the Robinson House, where he had fought his first battle 13 months earlier and paused with other artillery units to await orders. Toward sunset orders arrived to hurry artillery to the right flank of Jackson's position, which anchored along a railroad cut, paralleling the Warrenton Pike.

Pelham later noted: "I took three pieces at a gallop through a thick woods . . . bearing to the right of the troops in position (Ewell's division). I crossed the old railroad about 1 mile from Groveton and took position between it and the turnpike. . . . I moved on at a gallop until a heavy volley of musketry apprised me of the enemy's presence. I immediately put my guns in position and engaged them at about 50 or 60 yards. We continued the fight for an hour or more, when, our reinforcements coming up, we drove the enemy back." In the dash to get to his position in the twilight darkness, two of the three cannons were misdirected or temporarily lost, and the one Pelham ran into position

A marker cannon is just barely visible in the tall grass at Manassas National Battlefield along a battle ridge from the battle of Second Manassas. Pelham's shots surprised Union infantry marching along the road, since he used terrain to initially conceal his position. (skb)

had part of its limber pole temporarily broken. This damage forced Pelham and the gun crew to hold their position and continue "firing until the enemy were driven back," instead of withdrawing sooner.

The Union troops on the receiving side of Pelham's gun hailed from western states and were soon to be known as the "Iron Brigade," for their toughness in battle. Lt. Finney of the 19th Indiana Infantry described the evening artillery fire: "The unearthly sound of these fearful missiles struck terror to the stoutest heart; yet cool and collected stood that line, obeying with alacrity every command, and waiting impatiently for the order to advance. The order was given; shells burst in front, above, and behind, crashed through the branches of the tree, plowed up the ground, and yelled demoniacly through the air, yet steadily forward pressed the line." Union artillery countered Pelham's single gun, but he managed to shift positions enough to remain in the field until more Confederate support arrived. Jackson praised Pelham for "his services [which] were much needed."

On this opening day of the second battle of Manassas, Pelham's quick response and arrival had bought time for Jackson. The following morning, Pelham and his battery were on the opposite side of the battlefield, discouraging Union troops from advancing toward Sudley Mill and the rear of Jackson's line. Union cavalry threatened Jackson's supply train and medical ambulances, and Confederate cavalry and

A piece of high ground at the right flank of Jackson's line near Brawner's Farm; Pelham may have used this position as he fired on the (soon-to-be-named) Iron Brigade. (skb)

A sketch of Union infantry during the battle of Second Manassas. Formations of infantry made easy targets for Pelham's guns on this battlefield and others. (loc)

horse artillery reacted quickly. "The vigilant Pelham had unlimbered his battery and dispersed that portion of them which had reached the wood," Jackson later praised. Both Generals Lee and Stuart also noted Pelham's bravery and swift response, praising him for this action in their official reports. Stuart summarized his compliment by noting, "Captain Pelham, always at the right place at the right time, unlimbered his battery and soon dispersed that portion in the woods."

After driving off that Union threat, Pelham obeyed orders to move back toward the Confederate right, meeting Gen. Jackson along the way. According to Pelham, Jackson "ordered me to ride over the field with him; and after pointing out the different roads he gave me discretionary orders to engage my battery where fitting opportunity should occur." This directive reflects the trust that Jackson willingly placed in Pelham, essentially giving the young artillery captain the ability to move around the battlefield as needed for defense or offensive harassment.

Pelham fulfilled the confidence Jackson had in him. While Jackson's infantry fought to hold their position in and along the railroad cut and watched anxiously for signs of Longstreet's arrival through Thoroughfare Gap, Pelham spent the rest of August 29 eyeing the field. He shifted his cannons to effective points and dueling for nearly two hours with Union artillery near Grovetown, until he had only ammunition left for one cannon. Here, Pelham was "left alone, with one gun, exposed to the fire of a long line of batteries with a direct and flank fire," and—despite seeking permission to withdraw—was forced to stay for fifteen to twenty minutes and "until the trail of my only gun had been struck and shivered."

The Deep Cut of the Unfinished Railroad is visible in the right of this photograph. Jackson's Confederate infantry defended this position during the battle of Second Manassas. (skb)

Looking from the Union perspective, up the sloping ground toward the Railroad Cut on the Second Manassas battlefield. (skb)

Once off the firing line, Pelham "moved my battery to the rear to procure ammunition, but could only get a very limited supply." Sunset on August 29 found Jackson's Confederates still in their defensive position, with the cavalry continuing to watch the flanks; everyone anticipated the hoped-for arrival of Lee and Longstreet to bring much needed reinforcements and perhaps a surprise attack against Pope's army.

On August 30, Pelham "held my battery in readiness on the field for action, but it being the only battery of horse artillery, would be very much needed in case of a retreat or pursuit." Obediently, Pelham sat out the fight, conserving his ammunition as Jackson had ordered. For other soldiers, though, this day of battle proved decisive. Heavy Union attacks battered Jackson's infantry line again, but in the late afternoon the lead elements of Longstreet's corps burst onto

the field, catching Union divisions on the flank and pushing them into a hurried retreat. Once again, the Confederates had dominated victory at Manassas.

Another perspective of terrain near Brawner's Farm and where Pelham moved and fired his cannons during the opening hours of Second Manassas. (skb)

For Pelham, the battle of Second Manassas marked increased trust from Jackson, not just to arrive rapidly and hold a position, but to survey a battlefield and go into action with discretionary judgment. Lee, Jackson, and Stuart offered praise for Pelham's decisions and fighting during this battle, making him a noticeable officer in the triumphant army. In his notes and report from this battle, Pelham particularly noted the courage of his men, mentioning some by name, but then adding "every non-commissioned officer and private acted so gallantly I cannot particularize." He also proudly mentioned the artillery skill shown in his battery. "The accuracy with which my guns were fired and the rapidity with which they were served during both days was very gratifying, and the execution they wrought was very great." But gallantry had a price; at least six artillerymen had fallen, one killed and five reported wounded.

Battle was not theatrics for Pelham. Certainly, the horse artillery style of fighting had flair, speed, and often dramatic positions, but he took pride in

Union veterans created this monument near the Deep Cut and dedicated it in June 1865.
(skb)

the effectiveness and training of his battery. He had prepared them, and now they performed—making a difference toward victory for the Confederates.

As Pope's army retreated toward Washington City, Jackson looked for another way to hasten their retreat and strike another blow. With the assistance of Stuart's cavalry, Jackson's corps made a flank march, and troops engaged at the battle of Chantilly on September 1, 1862. Pelham and his cannons were once again in the forefront, helping to clear Yankees off the turnpikes and holding key positions until the infantry arrived. The heavy summer rainstorms made their tasks difficult as mud dragged at the cannon wheels.

Union troops continued their retreat after another defeat at Chantilly. Stuart, with cavalry and horse artillery, kept pursuing, and the cavalry general later reported:

The enemy have retired, Fairfax Court-House was occupied by Lee's brigade, and I sent Hampton's brigade . . . to attack the enemy at Flint Hill. Getting several pieces of the Stuart Horse Artillery in position, Brigadier-General Hampton opened on the enemy at that point, and our sharpshooters advancing about the same time, after a brief engagement the enemy hastily retired. They were immediately pursued, and Captain Pelham, having chosen a new position, again opened upon them with telling effect, scattering them in every direction.

"The Horse Artillery has won imperishable laurels," Stuart bragged, but more glory lay ahead on roads that stretched northward into Maryland and Pennsylvania.

Though the enemy to his immediate front had been scattered, plenty of Union troops had escaped Manassas to fight another day. Pope's army and McClellan's force (now returned from the Peninsula) united with "Little Mac" in command. A combined and strong Army of the Potomac would now oppose the Confederates' next move, and Lee already planned to leave defensive strikes and take the war into the heart of Maryland. Stuart's cavalry with Pelham's battery would play a key role in success as Confederate infantry spread out over a network of roads to turn northward.

Antietam:
"The corn field . . . full of Yankees"

CHAPTER NINE

The Potomac River marked a boundary, and for the first time, Pelham crossed onto northern soil as an invader. The crossing at White's Ford on September 5, 1862, was the first of several trespasses that the Stuart Horse Artillery made in the autumn weeks as the cavalrymen and Pelham's cannons carried war into Maryland. The Confederate cavalry's arrival in the border state opened the doors for the infantry as the horsemen cleared the roads, scouted, skirmished, and kept watch on the Union forces.

Horse artillery required rapid movement, and Pelham kept up with the demands of his battery. On September 6, he requested and received 28 new horses to replace the equine casualties from Second Manassas. Supply and readiness occupied Pelham's attention, one of the less glamorous roles of command that ensured the success of his battery.

Like many units arriving in Maryland, the Stuart Horse Artillery had some moments of fun and plentiful food. Some artillerymen killed a pig, claiming it had been in self-defense when they had

According to some accounts, Pelham slept in the "shelter" of a fence on the eve of the battle of Antietam until Stuart woke him and told him to check the placements of the cannons on Nicodemus Heights. (skb)

This painting of John Pelham at the Court House Annex in Richmond depicts him leaning forward as if sighting a cannon or observing a battle scene. (loc)

been attacked in the night; Pelham apparently asked no questions. Another food incident was smellier when "At a point on the B&O Railroad, a lot of whiskey and salt fish fell into our hands. Rubber buckets and camp kettles were filled, and hung onto the gun carriages, and the contents sloshed out as we proceeded. The men made a grotesque appearance as they munched the fish and washed it down with the beverage, and some of them imbibing too freely were in a hilarious mood, and felt able to aniholate the enemy at once."

Hilarity and confidence soared around Stuart's headquarters, too. Pelham almost certainly participated in the spur-of-the-moment dance that Stuart allowed his staff to organize on the evening of September 8. Hosted at a large, former academy in Urbana, this party gathered civilian Southern sympathizers for a dance, complete with a decorated room and music provided by the 18th Mississippi Infantry's band. However, determined Union cavalry interrupted the lively dancing, and officers hurried out the door, galloping into the darkness to fight. Staff officer Heros Von Borcke claimed that Pelham summoned multiple cannon and helped in the night's repulse. Following the fight, many of the officers returned to the ballroom to reassure the women and continue the dance—as the legendary accounts claim.

Pelham slips through the pages of primary sources during the Maryland Campaign, leaving blanks in the knowledge of his exact places, experiences, or thoughts. He turned 24 on September 7, the day before the Urbana Ball. He also received a promotion to major. On September 12, near Frederick, Maryland, Stuart wrote to his wife, giving updates on the cavalry and officers, and he noted: "Pelham is a Major," indicating the news of his promotion had arrived from Richmond. Life had taken turns Pelham had not expected, but his position as a Confederate artillery officer seemed secure. Given enough ammunition, he seemed ready to take on whatever dangers and challenges galloped his way.

As the Maryland Campaign unfolded, Confederate cavalry ranged through southern Maryland, screening and scouting for the infantry columns spread over miles of roads and pursuing varying objectives according to Lee's orders. Cavalry positioned along the ridges, passes, and roads leading through Catoctin Mountain, Sugar Loaf, and South Mountain, trying to slow Union advance to the west toward the divided Confederates.

A rumor claims Union troops captured Pelham on September 13, while he worked with Gen. Fitzhugh Lee. However, Pelham made an escape, cut through the lines, and returned to his Confederate friends on September 14. This intriguing incident fell into the historic shadows of the battle of South Mountain on September 14.

Using the passes of South Mountain as defensive positions, Stuart tried to delay and prevent Union troops from crossing this geographical point. Jackson's corps clustered around Harpers Ferry, forcing that city and Union garrison to surrender, while Longstreet's corps ranged to Hagerstown. If the Union army caught the Confederate divided, the Yankees might score an easier victory or a military advantage. South Mountain served as a natural barrier to block the Union columns.

Pelham and guns of the Stuart Horse Artillery fought at Fox's Gap during the battle of South Mountain. (skb)

Stuart's cavalry had retreated into the gaps of South Mountain on September 14, and some Confederate infantry had also arrived. Col. Thomas Rosser, with the 5th Virginia Cavalry and a section of Pelham's Battery, rode to Fox's Gap. The former West Point roommates now fought together in a mountain pass in Maryland. Rosser had his troopers dismount and placed them behind a protective stonewall. Pelham positioned cannon to the left of Rosser's line and, as the battle opened on September 15, dueled with Battery E of the 2nd U.S. Artillery. Union and Confederate infantry came into the fight, and the cavalry and horse artillery fell back. Throughout the day, Pelham continued to support Rosser, and their concerted efforts kept the Old Sharpsburg Road in Confederate hands for a short time. However, in the night, the Confederates withdrew, and Pelham took his battery through Boonsboro, fired on Union pursuers near Keedysville, and then headed south toward Antietam Creek, crossing at the Middle Bridge.

By September 16, the Confederates formed battle lines on the southwest side of Antietam Creek. Pelham and the Stuart Horse Artillery rolled into position on Nicodemus Heights, a piece of high ground anchoring the left of Jackson's line and covering the Hagerstown Pike. Stonewall's chief of artillery, Stapleton Crutchfield, remained in Harpers Ferry, organizing captured artillery.

A small NPS sign along Maryland Route 65 points to the vicinity of the Nicodemus House. Civilian women and children dashed from that structure on the morning of September 17, 1862, as an artillery duel crashed. Pelham ordered his gunners to cease fire and sent officers to bring the civilians to a safer location. (skb)

Stuart and Pelham oversaw organizing and placing all the artillery batteries on Nicodemus Heights, an important position supporting Jackson's line. By nightfall on September 16, Union troops had advanced toward Nicodemus Heights, and a brief artillery duel ensued. Then the fields fell silent, each side knowing the other's position, but neither attempting further fighting that rainy night.

Pelham slept in a haystack near a rail fence, only to be awakened in the drizzly darkness by Gen. Stuart. "My dear fellow, don't you know that the corn field at the foot of the hill is full of Yankees? and that you ought to have your guns in position now, for if you wait until daylight the hill will be swarming with blue coats." Roused, Pelham spent the remain hours inspecting the placement of the batteries and using the uneven terrain of Nicodemus Heights to his advantage. Along with the Stuart Horse Artillery, Pelham commanded the Staunton, Alleghany, Danville, and D'Aquin's Louisiana Guard Artillery batteries, which Jackson had sent to the position. At least 15 cannons poised on

As of 2024, the Nicodemus Farm is privately owned, including the artillery positions at Nicodemus Heights. All the photos included in this chapter taken on the farm were taken during a tour and with permission. Please do not attempt to access the property without permission! (skb)

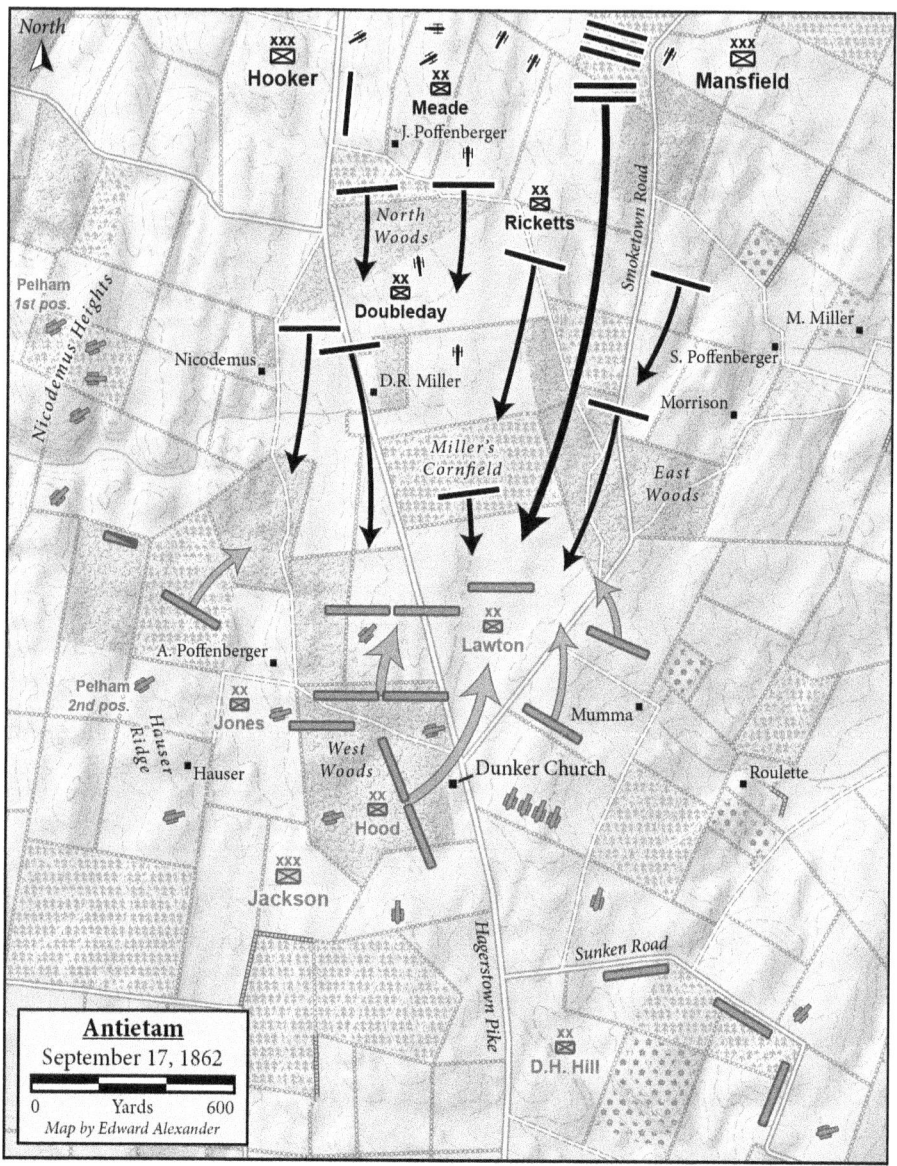

ANTIETAM—Pelham's quick actions during the battle of Antietam moved Confederate artillery out of direct danger of capture and then returned them to key high ground as the battle lines shifted.

the heights as morning light dawned across the rolling terrain that would become some of the bloodiest landscape in America in the next hours.

The opening shots of the battle of Antietam echoed from Nicodemus Heights, blasting into the Union infantry moving through Miller's Cornfield. Union artillery fire countered, but Pelham had used the terrain and the reverse slope of Nicodemus

This sketch shows Confederate troops fighting in the woods near Dunker Church. Pelham directed artillery fire toward the West Woods as the infantry fight shifted around Dunker Church and into these woods, trying to stop the Union advance. (loc)

Heights to his advantage, making it hard for Union gunners to find the Confederate cannons. Pelham probably did not know it, but that morning he exchanged shots with Brig. Gen. Henry J. Hunt, Chief of Artillery for the Army of the Potomac and one of the foremost artillerymen in American military ranks. During this morning, artillery duel, civilians at the Nicodemus House ran out of the dwelling and across ploughed fields, putting themselves in greater danger while trying to escape. Both sides ordered a ceasefire until the women and children arrived safely in the Confederate lines.

Pelham's position on Nicodemus Heights allowed him to engage with Union batteries and blast Union infantry in the Cornfield and edge of North Woods. Artillery and small arms projectiles laid the corn and

September 17, 1862, became the bloodiest single day in U.S. history. Thousands of dead and wounded soldiers in blue and gray lay along the roads and in the fields when the battle of Antietam ended. (loc)

ranks of men flat, and Union soldiers later wrote about the fierce, unrelenting fire bursting on their right flanks from the unreachable heights.

As the morning battle shifted, Union troops pushed toward West Woods and Dunker Church. The Confederate infantry fell back and charged forward, but the overall lines shifted and Pelham's guns on Nicodemus Heights risked capture. Acting quickly, Pelham ordered the batteries to retreat to Hauser Ridge, which sat behind West Woods and covered his ammunition supply line and a route toward the Potomac River. The new position on Hauser Ridge supported the hard-pressed Confederate infantry in West Woods, and when Union troops broke through, they experienced "the most terrific fire of grape and canister."

When the Union attacks near the Woods and Dunker Church eased and the heavy fighting shifted to other portions of the Confederate line, Pelham and Stuart moved the cannon again. Using a "leap frog" pattern of firing and moving, they paralleled retreating Union soldiers along the high ground and repositioned on Nicodemus Heights, securing the Confederate left flank again.

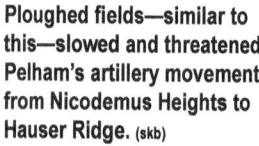

Ploughed fields—similar to this—slowed and threatened Pelham's artillery movement from Nicodemus Heights to Hauser Ridge. (skb)

During the movement to and from Hauser Ridge, the ploughed fields slowed and sometimes halted Pelham's movements, but infantry support came to the artillery's aid. Samuel Buck of the 13th Virginia

Infantry remembered: "I had the honor of fighting by his side at Sharpsburg, when the Thirteenth [Virginia] supported his batteries on our left. . . . The horses could not drag the heavy guns over the plowed field, and the men of that grand old regiment almost carried the pieces to a position only a few hundred yards in front of the enemy, and Pelham loaded each gun with double charges and kept thousands of the enemy back."

Toward the end of September 17, Pelham took the artillery on an offensive movement. Lee ordered Jackson to gather cavalry and some infantry to prepare for an attack launched from the Confederate left flank. Pelham would advance and test the Union position and firepower. Against the protests of the battery commanders, Pelham ordered them forward, laughingly saying, "Oh, we must stir them up a little and then slip away." He received reinforcement with Capt. William Poague, who explained: "Along with six or eight other guns, under the direction of Maj. Pelham, an attempt was made to dislodge the enemy's batteries, but failed completely, being silenced in fifteen or twenty minutes by a most terrific fire from a

Looking toward the high ground of Nicodemus Heights where Pelham initially placed cannons under his expanded command on the morning of the battle of Antietam. Using the reverse slope (back slope, away from the enemy) to his advantage, Pelham gained a little protection for his gunners. (skb)

The Potomac River near the ford at Shepherdstown was the scene of fighting and escape as the Confederate army retreated after the battle of Antietam. (skb)

number of the enemy's batteries." The Union artillery line was too strong, and while Pelham probably knew that from the beginning, he followed Lee and Jackson's orders without public complaint and proved that further Confederate attack here would be futile.

Survivors on both sides stared in horror as twilight descended. Nearly 23,000 men were dead, wounded, or missing. They waited to see if large-scale fighting would resume on September 18, but when it did not, Confederate infantry, artillery, and cavalry prepared to retreat to the Potomac River and back into Virginia.

The fight at Antietam tested Pelham's skill in handling a larger artillery command, and he successfully carried out his assignment. Throughout the day, Pelham—supported by Stuart—used a series of conventional and unconventional methods of artillery fighting. He borrowed tactics of the Horse Artillery and used them with regular batteries, having them move position suddenly and rapidly for either more advantageous fire power or battery protection.

Stuart noted, "The gallant Pelham displayed all those noble qualities which have made him immortal. He had under his command batteries from every portion of General Jackson's command. The batteries . . . did splendid service, as also did the Stuart Horse Artillery, all under Pelham. The hill, held on the extreme left so long and so gallantly by artillery alone, was essential to the maintenance of our position."

When necessity forced Jackson to hand over the guns to Stuart and Pelham, another military partnership emerged. Stuart might have seemed like an unlikely choice for an acting chief of artillery, but his experience in protecting flanks, paired with Pelham's expertise with the guns created a stunningly successful operation. The ability to handle artillery and change plans and positions rapidly as the battle unfolded hallmarked the Confederate artillery on Jackson's flank in this battle. These were tactics Stuart and Pelham had spent months perfecting on other battlefields.

Though a future battle in 1862 would be hailed as the zenith of Pelham's artillery career, his actions on the high ground of Nicodemus Heights are perhaps his largest success and contribution toward a Confederate battlefield victory. The guns under Pelham's command secured and held the Confederate left flank in a desperate, large-scale battle. As one friend later wrote: "At Sharpsburg he had command of nearly all the artillery on our left, and directed it with the hand of a master."

Raiding Chambersburg:
"Tax upon one's endurance"

CHAPTER TEN

Rest eluded Major Pelham. The Army of Northern Virginia had retreated into Virginia while the Stuart Horse Artillery formed part of the rearguard. On September 19, Lee sent the cavalry riding north to Williamsport, attempting to convince McClellan that the Confederates had not tamely finished the Maryland Campaign. The cavalry recrossed the Potomac at Williamsport and clashed with Union cavalry in the streets of the riverside village. According to a traditional account, an enthused female tried to join the horse artillery at Williamsport, and the young teenager refused to leave until Pelham let her fire a cannon. Despite the artillery's temporary reinforcement, the Confederate cavalry faced heavy skirmishing as they advanced toward Hagerstown, and by nightfall, they fell back into Virginia, pursued by Yankees.

With the Maryland Campaign concluded, the Confederate cavalry set up patrol cordons through northwestern Virginia and entered a brief period of rest and refitting. Pelham accepted an invitation to visit

The Chambersburg Raid of 1862 took Pelham and Stuart's cavalry into the heart of southern Pennsylvania. Pelham's guns were threatening sights to the civilians in Chambersburg. (skb)

A historic cemetery sits on a bluff of high ground between the town of Williamsport and the C&O Canal and the Potomac River. Pelham may have used this high ground or other high ground nearby as he fired at Union forces at Williamsport. (skb)

Ephraim Alburtis—his 1861 battery commander—in Martinsburg; Heros Von Borcke accompanied him to the dinner and added his tales to the entertainment. Alburtis delighted in hearing stories about Pelham and later told an interviewer, "Why—that boy—he hadn't changed a bit! He was just exactly the same as when he came to my battery! And, good Lord, how he did blush when Major von Borcke told us all about him!"

Pelham had new responsibilities in the wake of the Maryland Campaign and his promotion to major. The Stuart Horse Artillery had increased to five batteries: the First Stuart Horse Artillery commanded by James Breathed, the Second Stuart Horse Artillery with Mathis W. Henry, and new batteries with Roger P. Chew, James F. Hart, and Marcellus N. Moorman. Now, there were 22 guns total in the command—a mix of Blakeleys, Napoleons, and a few leftover Howitzers.

After Stuart established tented headquarters at "The Bower," owned by prominent citizen Adam Stephen Dandridge on September 28, the social life improved. Maj. Pelham found time from his duties to show off the guns to local admirers. According to Pvt. H. H. Matthews:

Pelham [brought] the ladies over to our camp, showing the guns and the men under his command. He seemed to be so proud of them. From gun to gun he would go, petting each piece as affectionately as if they were animals. He would tell the history of each gun—how at a certain place a particular gun had wrought such terrible execution among the Yankees, and so on to the end.

At "The Bower," according to WW Blackford, "Our General was the life of the party but he was ably seconded by von Borcke, Pelham and others of his staff, together with officers of cavalry regiments encamped near by. . . ." John E. Cooke, a relative of the Dandridge family, and cousin of Stuart's wife remembered that Pelham "seemed to spend some of his happiest hours" at "the old hall on the banks of the Opequon" where "all were charmed with his kind temper and his sunny disposition; with his refinement, his courtesy, his high breeding, and simplicity. Modest to a fault . . . he became a favourite with all around him. . . ."

The idyllic setting and company briefly disguised war, but the splendor of autumn hinted at approaching winter. The Confederate cavalry needed horses, and McClellan's Union army needed a rousing scare—according to Stuart's planning.

Selecting 1,800 cavalrymen and horses and four cannons from the horse artillery, Stuart prepared for one of his most daring feats. The picked men and horses had been pulled from their regiments for their skill and equine condition, forming a type of special force as they headed deep into enemy territory. The raiders assembled at Darkesville, Virginia (now West Virginia) on October 9, and then rode to Hedgesville.

On October 10, 1862, at sunrise, the cavalry column crossed the Potomac River at McCoy's Ford and rode north through the narrow distance of Maryland, capturing a signal station along the way. Once in Pennsylvania—a firmly Union state, unlike

The Chambersburg Raid was Stuart's second ride around McClellan's army in 1862, but Union cavalry responded quicker and with more boldness, hinting that Stuart's "joy rides" would not go unthreatened in the future. (loc)

McCoy's Ferry was the crossing point of the Potomac River for Stuart's raid into Pennsylvania in October 1862. (skb)

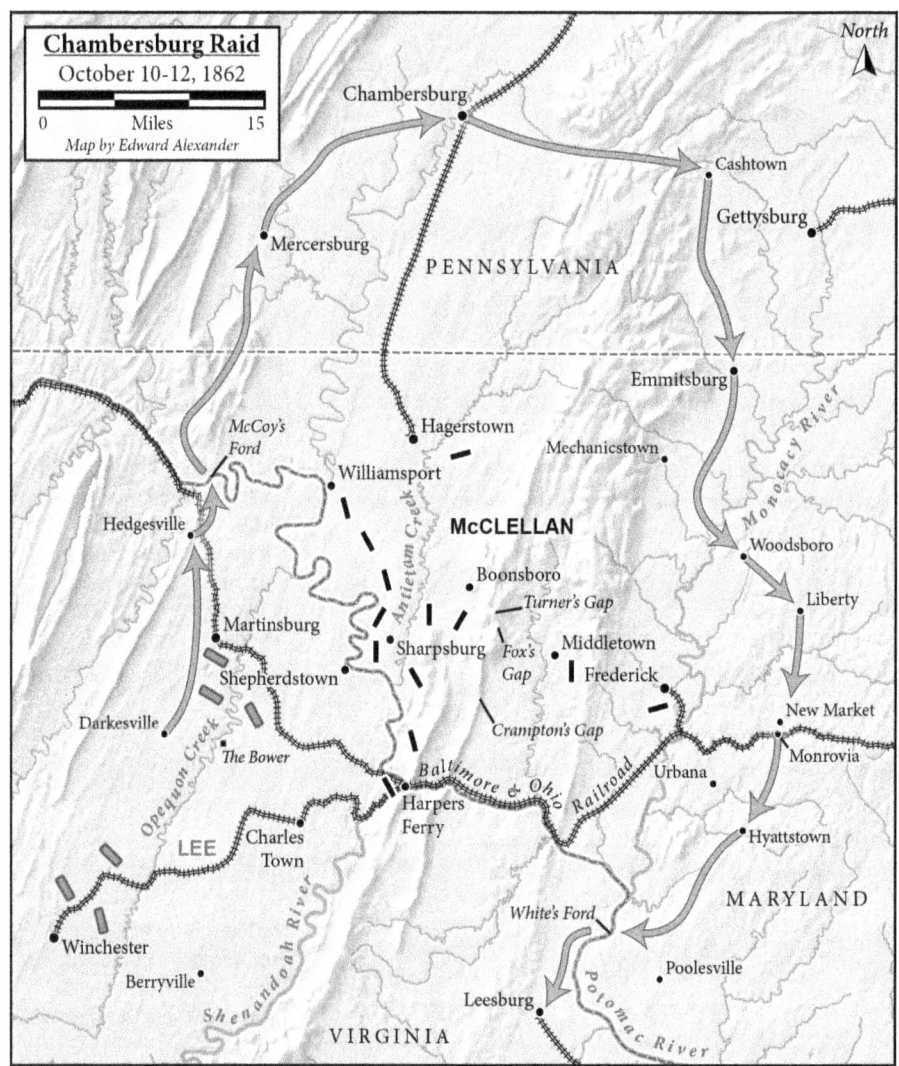

CHAMBERSBURG RAID—The Chambersburg Raid tested the endurance of Stuart's cavalry and horse artillery.

border state Maryland—the cavalrymen began taking horses from the farms and foraging for food. At this point in the raid, some of the Confederates impersonated Union troopers or merely did not correct the farmers' assumptions as they walked off with horses needed by the army for "their cause." Many of the horses were larger draft horses, not necessarily stamina horses for cavalry but strong for pulling cannon, and Pelham picked new animals for his teams.

Around noon, they reached Mercersburg, Pennsylvania. Rolling two cannon into the town square,

Pelham helped Stuart persuade the locals to accept Confederate money in exchange for shoes and boots. A staff officer captured a local map, literally taking it from a parlor wall, and they prepared to ride on. In Mercersburg, the horse artillery procured "straw hats, the kind usually worn by farmers in that region of Pennsylvania." The fashion choice prompted some teasing from Gen. Stuart, and one artilleryman recalled: "The appearance of the battery was grotesque, indeed, so that Gen. Stuart on riding through the battery asked Pelham where he got all the farmers from the name farmer stuck to us for quite a while. The constant rain had the tendency to make our hats quite limp, so that they resembled Shaker bonnets."

Stuart learned Union troops were rallying to cut him off at Hagerstown and decided to turn east instead of heading to that supply town. Chambersburg, Pennsylvania, lay about 20 miles to the northeast and was another major supply hub. Across the farmland

Pelham placed cannon in the town square at Mercersburg, adding a visible threat to Stuart's words and requests. (skb)

This sketch depicts the arrival of Confederate cavalry in Chambersburg. Note the civilians in the foreground. Some civilians were taken hostage during the raid and forced to go to Virginia. (loc)

The historic town square in Chambersburg, Pennsylvania, saw the arrival of Confederate cavalry. Here, Stuart began to surmise the difficulties his column would have as they turned back toward Maryland and Virginia. (skb)

of Pennsylvania, the gray-clad horsemen met frowns, deceit, and minor resistance as they headed toward Chambersburg. The rainy weather made muddy roads, and Pelham and his artillerymen frequently had to halt and change tired horses.

After a ride of approximately 40 miles in one day, the buildings of Chambersburg appeared in the misty evening. Unsure if the town was garrisoned or abandoned by enemy forces, Pelham positioned two cannons on a rise of ground overlooking the town, prepared to help with negotiations. But the local civilians agreed to surrender, and Stuart occupied the town, cut telegraph lines, failed to destroy the nearby trestle bridge, and took prominent citizens hostage. In the night, a telegraph message got out of Chambersburg before the Confederates cut the line; McClellan and the governor of Pennsylvania knew that Stuart and 1,800 cavalry were deep in Union territory. Stuart realized Union troops reacted across Pennsylvania and Maryland, and he could be easily cut off if they moved with uncharacteristic speed. The race back to Virginia had begun.

The next morning—October 11—the cavalrymen destroyed warehouses of supplies in Chambersburg, railroad cars, and several machine shops. Stuart wanted to head toward Leesburg, Virginia, but throughout the day, he had to alter his route to keep his objective secret and to change course as Union cavalry gathered more quickly than he had anticipated. Heading east, Stuart aimed for Gettysburg, then intentionally missed that town,

and swung south toward Emmitsburg, Maryland, where "we were hailed by the inhabitants with the most enthusiastic demonstrations of joy." Stuart determined to ride through the night, instructing Pelham and the other officers to not to stop for anything or anybody.

After crossing the Monocacy River, the cavalry column continued, passing through Liberty, New Market, and Monrovia, with a quick pause at the Baltimore & Ohio Railroad to disrupt communication and transportation. Pelham struggled with weary horses, and on one slippery, steep road, he nearly lost two cannons down a slope. Staff officer Henry McClellan noted, "Horses for the guns and caissons there were in abundance; and as fast as one team was broken down the horses were turned out and others were substituted. Three or four times during the night did the drivers change their horses, and the march was made without delay or interruption."

The column had gone 65 miles in 20 hours, after leaving Chambersburg. Exhaustion overtook the cavalrymen, and W. W. Blackford wrote descriptively of the experience: "It is no small tax upon one's endurance to remain marching all night; during the day there is always something to attract the attention and amuse, but at night there is nothing.

Illustrations of Chambersburg during the 1862 Raid; some supply buildings were burned and Confederates took supplies from the shops and warehouses, too. (loc)

The monotonous jingle of arms and accoutrements mingles with the tramp of horses' feet into a drowsy hum all along the marching column, which makes one extremely sleepy, and to be sleepy and not to be allowed to sleep is exquisite torture."

At Hyattstown, just before daylight on October 12, Stuart discovered McClellan had moved his army supply wagons and sent out a few thousand Union cavalry commanded to guard the Potomac River fords.

A sharp fight at Poolesville, with one of Pelham's guns provided covering fire, allowed the Confederate column to slip toward the Potomac River and White's Ford.

While most of the cavalry headed into the ford, Pelham and a few detachments of horsemen formed the rearguard. "Pelham pounded away with two guns first one side and then the other, with great spirit, on the heads of their columns." The lone gun held back the Union troopers until the last of the Confederates had reached the river, holding "an open gap . . . for us to pass through." As soon as the last of the raiders reached the ford and he received the signal, Pelham and his crew limbered their gun and "rumbling along . . . into the water. We were not half across when the bank we had left was swarming with the enemy who opened a galling fire upon us, the bullets splashing the water around us like a shower of rain. But the guns from the Virginia side immediately opened on them and mitigated their fire considerably, and we soon crossed and stood once more on Virginia soil."

The southern Pennsylvania countryside provided rich raiding ground for Stuart's cavalry, especially as they collected horses to take back to Virginia and into cavalry service. (skb)

Back in Virginia, the exhausted Confederates rode west, back to their camps near Winchester and "The Bower." The Chambersburg Raid resulted in only a few wounded Confederates, but weary survivors fell from their saddles and slept along the road after reaching Virginia. This Second Ride Around McClellan totaled 126 miles in three days, with most of the distance accomplished as a forced march. The Confederates hauled 1,200 captured horses back to Virginia along with 30 prominent civilian prisoners who would be exchanged for captured Confederates and destroyed an estimated $250,000 of property along their route, mostly in Chambersburg. With hindsight, some cavalrymen wondered if it was worth the risk and effort; the captured horses and the selected men and horses returned so exhausted and run down it took significant time for recovery.

Pelham had missed the First Ride Around McClellan on the Peninsula, but he held a prime place in the history of the Second Ride. Covering the retreat and holding open the escape route to White's Ford allowed the Confederate cavalry column to return safely to Virginia. Stuart and the other officers and troopers gratefully recognized Pelham's role in their escape and success.

Returning to "The Bower," Stuart and his raiders received a warm welcome from the Dandridge family and other local civilians. The cavalry officers organized a dance on October 15 to celebrate their success. The autumn night of music and frivolity morphed the difficulties of the Chambersburg Raid into a legend. "Oh ye huge shady trees along the rippling banks of the moonlit Opequan! How many tales ye could tell of those . . . days," mused one witness later. Hints that Pelham had fallen in love with a young woman during the days at "The Bower" drift through the accounts of several staff officers—never quite clear, just swirling in their stories like the October leaves. (See Appendix A). Maybe John E. Cooke said it best, "When [Pelham] left the haunts of 'The Bower,' I think he regretted it. But work called him."

The Potomac River near White's Ferry (looking from the Virginia side); at White's Ferry, Pelham held off Union cavalry while Confederate horsemen escaped across the river. He eventually made his own escape, bringing the last cannon and gun crew with him, safely to the Virginia shore. (skb)

Union cavalry moved into Northern Virginia, and Pelham's guns would welcome along the lanes of Loudoun County. Romance—if it had started or continued—would have to wait. The pull of war and his concepts of duty took him back to combat, and with a last tug on the harness or saddle straps, a quick order, and spurring, Pelham rode toward his next battles.

Loudoun Valley Campaign:
"Aimed a gun and fought with his men"

CHAPTER ELEVEN

The cavalry bugles echoed into the Shenandoah Valley, calling troopers and horse artillery men to ride forward. McClellan's army roused from its rest and started crossing the Potomac River into Northern Virginia on October 26, 1862. Stuart's cavalry, despite strong morale, was in a critical situation with disease eating at the horses' hoofs, reducing the number of mounted men who could fight. But the cavalry had to provide a screen for the moving infantry.

Lee split his infantry, sending Longstreet's Corps over the Blue Ridge Mountains and toward Culpeper in Central Virginia while Jackson's Corps consolidated around Winchester, safeguarding the Shenandoah Valley and ready to move in response to the Federals. Meanwhile, Stuart's cavalry formed a screen and a connection in northern Virginia, preventing a Union surprise toward Jackson or a quick dash at Longstreet and also blocking Union troops from getting between the Confederate army wings and slowing down the march. A Confederate cavalryman summed up the late autumn weeks of military duty: "The cavalry was

John Pelham reportedly etched his name on this glass window that overlooks the porch of Welbourne. Today, there is still an etching in the windowpane, but it is difficult to photograph. (skb)

A ford in Loudoun County where Pelham's guns crossed the creek. Much of Loudoun County is still rural and the roads, pathways, fields, and woods are easy to imagine as the scenes of cavalry and artillery. (skb)

ordered to cross the Blue Ridge at 'Snicker's Gap,' and retard his movements. So, we were in one continual skirmish almost day and night for some 20 days, from the Potomac to the Rapidan. . . . We generally held our own until they come with over whelming force. We were ably assisted and helped in our efforts by 'Pelham's Battery' of horse artillery."

On October 27, Pelham and Capt. Farley, one of Stuart's scouts, spent the evening at Welbourne, the Dulany Family's elegant home in Loudoun County. One of the Dulany girls wrote to her mother about the military visitors, adding, "Major Pelham . . . is an Alabamian about twenty one or two, a graduate of West Point, and so bright and intelligent, you could hardly believe in looking at his youthful face and figure that he ranked as Major. What a pleasant evening that was, I wonder if I shall ever see my two acquaintances again. . . . While at the breakfast table, the distant report of a cannon was heard, followed by another and another. "There go your guns, Pelham," said Capt. Farley, and as the steady firing continued, they requested Uncle Richard to order their horses. . . ." The fight across Loudoun County began, and some of Pelham's finest moments of horse artillery tactics and personal heroics occurred during this campaign.

On October 30, Stuart took part of his cavalry, crossed the Blue Ridge Mountains at Snicker's Gap, and entered Loudoun County. Pelham joined this movement, taking six artillery pieces, and meeting Union resistance near the village of Aldie. Union troopers—improving their cavalry tactics and gaining confidence—pushed the Confederate regiments out of the town and sent Stuart scrambling to find Pelham. A staff officer found the young major, seated on a huge draft horse and with his stirrups set too short, forcing his knees into a tight posture. Pelham assured the worried officer that the batteries were coming up with all haste, but they had not been able to keep pace with the galloping cavalrymen. Selecting a position, Pelham put two guns into action and started dueling with Union artillery, eventually forcing the bluecoats to fall back. However, Stuart also withdrew to Middleburg, avoiding more Union cavalry approaching his rear.

On November 2, the cavalries clashed again, this time near the hamlet of Union, modern day Unison. Here, Stuart reported "the Stuart Horse Artillery, under the incomparable Pelham, supported by the cavalry sharpshooters, made a gallant and obstinate resistance, maintaining their ground for the great part of the day, both suffering heavily, one of our caissons exploding from the enemy's shot."

This church in the village of Unison has Civil War graffiti inside and stands across from a field where Pelham placed cannons during the fighting near the village. (skb)

It was during this engagement that Major Pelham conducted a howitzer some distance beyond support to a neighboring hill and opened a masked fire upon a body of the enemy's cavalry in the valley beneath, putting them to flight, capturing their flag and various articles—their arms, equipments, and horses, as well as some prisoners—sustaining in this extraordinary feat no loss whatever. The enemy finally enveloped our position with his superior numbers, both infantry and cavalry, so as to compel our withdrawal; but every hill-top and every foot of ground was disputed, so that the enemy made progress of less than a mile during the day. The enemy were held at bay until dark at Seaton's Hill, which they assailed with great determination, but each time signally repulsed by the well-directed fire of the Horse Artillery. Major Pelham, directing one of the shots himself at the color-bearer of an infantry regiment, struck him down at a distance of 800 yards.

Stuart's description of the fight near Union focuses on the outcomes, but other accounts suggest that Pelham's anger flared during this battle. In a rare instance, Union guns forced him to move, and he could not prevent their deadly destruction wreaking his men, horses, and equipment. The death that Pelham's orders often dealt to his enemy was now returned to him. He saw the exploding caisson and several of his artillerymen torn to pieces, dead instantly or mortally wounded. These scenes of carnage and the cries of his wounded prompted Pelham to grab the howitzer and a small crew and gallop into an advanced position. He loaded the howitzer with double-canister and waited for his enemy to come close to his hidden position before blasting the Union infantry. Like the story from First Manassas, Pelham aimed and shot down a flag—a verifiable fact from the 7th Indiana Infantry Regiment in the fighting near Union. Stuart allowed Pelham's revenge since it was effective. However, should the commander of five batteries of horse artillery have been dashing into a far-forward, exposed position to fire off a few shots? Was Pelham in his proper place for command or letting the emotion or opportunity of a moment drive his decisions?

Despite Pelham's heroics and hard fighting from other Confederate units, they were forced to retreat. Along Pantherskin Creek, Pelham and his artillerymen bivouacked and tried to rest, rousing partway through the night to position their guns as scouts confirmed Union soldiers creeping into a nearby cornfield. An early morning barrage mowed down the corn and warned the Union troops. Later that morning, Stuart intentionally split his force to better coordinate with moving Confederate infantry. The fighting in Loudoun Valley continued and shifted closer to Upperville as the day passed. Just beyond that village, Pelham placed six cannons on high ground and attempted to

Open fields near the village of Unison where Pelham and guns of the Stuart Horse Artillery fought advancing Union troops during the Loudoun Campaign. (skb)

slow the swiftly advancing Union forces. Von Borcke later remembered: "He skillfully covered our retreat, and, by the accuracy and rapidity of his firing, saved us from greater disaster. My brave friend was himself hard at work in his shirt sleeves, taking a hand with the cannoneers in loading and aiming the pieces."

The famous, historic stone walls in Loudoun County have been standing along the roads and fields for decades, many dating back to the Civil War years or older. (skb)

On November 4, Pelham joined Tom Rosser, acting as rearguard for his old West Point roommate as they maneuvered south. Union cavalry followed, eager but wary. They knew Pelham by sight and by firing tactics now, and as one Union trooper noted that morning, Pelham had "put on his fighting clothes." With intense calm, Pelham positioned cannons, called for ammunition, and ordered the firing that halted Union troopers just yards away from the Confederate line. Then, he directed the guns to be moved, and the process repeated, holding off the attackers and covering Rosser's retreat to reunite with other Confederate cavalry. At one point, Pelham was nearly surrounded, but he held, repositioned, fired, and above the commands and blasts the men of his Napoleon detachment sang "The Marseillaise."

On November 5, Pelham joined Capt. Henry and the guns of the Second Stuart Horse Artillery on the road to Barbee's Crossroads. Stuart had ordered the cavalry to return to this crossroads, and the horse artillery guns were among the first units to return. Here, a duel between Pelham and Henry against Pennington's horse artillery broke out, continuing for several hours. Still, at the end of the day, the Confederates retreated, Pelham again commanding the artillery rearguard.

High ground near Barbee's Crossroads where Pelham dueled with Union guns for several hours. (skb)

This post-war house constructed in Loudoun County is called "Pelham"— named after the Confederate officer by a young woman who seems to have had an especial fondness for stories of his exploits. (skb)

Over the next days, Pelham and his gunners fought at Waterloo Bridge, Amissville, Gaines's Cross Roads, and Newby's Cross Roads as early winter weather brought snow and sleet. By November 10, the Loudoun Valley Campaign ended, and the battered Confederate cavalry crossed the Hazel River. It had been a series of hard fights, but they had accomplished their mission by delaying the Union forces and protecting Confederate infantry's marching routes.

During one of the last artillery duels of the campaign, J. W. Bush, a Confederate sharpshooter, watched Pelham ready for yet another fight.

Upon the crest of the hill Major Pelham had placed a battery of four guns. . . . The wind was blowing from the northwest directly into our faces, and there was an occasional rift of snow. Pelham was mounted on a black horse, long and rakish, with keen round legs, beautiful neck and fiery eyes—every now and then he would put out one foot pawing the earth, then the other. Pelham was dressed in high top boots, a close-fitting gray overcoat with bright brass buttons, and buckskin gauntlets; a small sword hung by his side. His cheeks were rosy . . . with every appearance of a boy about sixteen years old. As we lay on the ground we looked up at him with the greatest admiration, because we knew he was every inch a soldier. Imagine this boy soldier fighting four pieces of artillery against eight. . . . In his anxiety he cried out: 'Tell General Stuart to cross his men, or I will not have a man left to work a gun!' He leaped from his horse, aimed a gun and fought with his men. Sometimes, when the Federal batteries would fire,

I would throw my face to the ground, expecting, when
I looked up, to see Major Pelham shot to fragments.

The historic Welbourne house still stands and is private property. Pelham and other Confederate officers stopped here and hoped for breakfast but were interrupted by nearby skirmishing at the start of the Loudoun Campaign. (skb)

Others went down with bad wounds, including one of the battery captains of the horse artillery, but Pelham escaped his battles unscathed. If he was ever injured, the hurt was minor enough to escape comment and major medical care.

Reflecting on the Loudoun Valley Campaign, Stuart noted in his official report Pelham had displayed "a skill and courage I have never seen surpassed." He praised the young major's "coup d'oeil" as "accurate and comprehensive, his choice of ground made with the eye of military genius, and his dispositions always such in retiring as to render it impossible for the enemy to press us without being severely punished for his temerity. His guns only retired from one position to assume another, and open upon the enemy with a fire so destructive that it threw their ranks into confusion and arrested their farther progress."

Commanders, peers, subordinates, observers, and enemies recognized Pelham's untiring courage and fighting skill in the Loudoun Valley Campaign. In many ways, this campaign marks the height of Pelham's success as a horse artillery commander, and his use of tactics and command for rapid, mobile artillery support and rearguard cover were stellar. The long ten days of fighting in November with classic horse artillery tactics and brutal rearguard action should be ranked as Pelham's most impressive military achievement. Stuart's success in this campaign came due to Pelham's skill.

Fredericksburg:
"You infernal, gallant fool, John Pelham!"

CHAPTER TWELVE

1862 drew to a close, and the Army of Northern Virginia faced the Army of the Potomac yet again. As if on predictable repeat, Stuart's cavalry ranged protectively around the Confederate army near Fredericksburg, Virginia, especially patrolling the lines of marching infantry and flanks. A combat scene emerged in rising mists and sunlight breaking during the battle of Fredericksburg on December 13. The opening moment in a panorama of war; the closing, memorable act of the year and a fight that would capture imagination in historical memory for decades.

Before the armies fought again, a few notable changes had occurred. On the Union side, Gen. Ambrose Burnside replaced McClellan, reorganized the Army of the Potomac, marched to the banks of the Rappahannock River, and waited opposite Fredericksburg for the arrival of his tardy pontoon bridges. Changes and command expansions also occurred for the Confederates. For Pelham, a fifth battery joined the Stuart Horse Artillery. Now, cannons could accompany each of the four cavalry brigades,

The battle of Fredericksburg and Pelham's daring opening shots on the morning of December 13, 1862, brought international fame to the young Confederate artillerist.
(skb)

General Ambrose Burnside, the reluctant commander of the Army of the Potomac at the end of 1862, revealed his crossing points of the Rappahannock River on December 11, then delayed on December 12, allowing the Confederates to assemble for the main day of battle on December 13. (loc)

and an extra battery operated as reserve, support, or advantageous opportunity. Captain Henry's battery attached to cavalry headquarters and was supposed to be the one closest to Pelham's immediate command.

Since Antietam, Stuart had been advocating for Pelham's promotion to lieutenant colonel. The general followed up with the war department as the fifth battery joined the Stuart Horse Artillery, explaining, "the position he holds [is] one of great responsibility, and it should have corresponding rank. I will add that Pelham's coolness, courage, ability and judgement, evinced on so many battle fields, vindicate his claims to promotion. So far as service goes he has long since won a colonelcy at the hands of his country."

Pelham probably had little time to worry about promotion, and the pattern of never-ending duties consumed his days in mid-November. Sick horses continued to plague the Confederate cavalry and horse artillery, but there was not yet time to take a rest.

Burnside's move to the Rappahannock prompted Lee to order Jackson to leave the Shenandoah Valley and march east. Stuart and the cavalry also joined the army near Fredericksburg. By early December, Confederate horsemen eyed the Rappahannock River, miles downstream from Fredericksburg, as they waited to confirm where Burnside intended to cross. Cavalry officers occasionally visited Gay Mont, the Bernard family's plantation home, and one of the young women noted in her diary, "Major Pelham also pleased us extremely, a mere youth apparently . . . slender almost to a fault, but quick & energetic in his movements & with an eagle eye that shows his spirit. He . . . looks like a man who would make his mark upon the world."

Supply wagons near Port Royal, Virginia. Notice how wide the Rappahannock River is here; this is near the location where Pelham fired on Union gunboats. (loc)

Pelham's defense attention was centered near Port Royal's riverfront. Four Union gunboats arrived near Port Royal on December 4. Forced downriver by some warning shots, the vessels steamed into a shoreline trap that Pelham had prepared with batteries of the Stuart Horse Artillery. A short duel ensued with the Confederate Blakelys blasting through one ship, and then return fire bursting canister onto one of the gun positions, wounding at least one Confederate artilleryman. Eventually, the Union gunboats moved further downstream and out of range. The incident received notable praise in the reports of superior officers.

Stuart's headquarters had welcomed a foreign visitor, Capt. Lewis Guy Phillips of the British Grenadier Guards, who liked to follow Pelham to examine the horse artillery and quiz him on preferred tactics. To show their guest some hospitable Southern fun, Pelham and some of Stuart's staff officers accepted an invitation to attend a dance at Chancellorsville, about 10 miles west of Fredericksburg on the evening of December 10. The journey to the welcoming house proved difficult along the freezing roads, and twice they wrecked the wagon. A battered set of officers arrived, decided to dance, and made their way back to Confederate lines the following morning before daybreak.

On December 11, Union engineers began building pontoon bridges at three crossing points near Fredericksburg. Confederate infantry and sharpshooters delayed their progress, and orders arrived for Jackson's corps and the cavalry to march toward Fredericksburg and extend Longstreet's defensive line. Union delays on December 12 gave the Confederates needed time to consolidate. Jackson's right flank anchored on Prospect Hill and stretched northward, connecting with Longstreet's infantry positioned along Telegraph Hill and Marye's Heights, directly west of the town of Fredericksburg. Stuart's cavalry positioned on Jackson's right flank, covering the lower ground south of Prospect Hill. The Lower Crossing allowed the Union's I and VI Corps to gather in Jackson's front.

This post-war illustration depicts Gen. Lee watching the battle of Fredericksburg. With a clear line of sight, Lee observed Pelham's flanking fire and spoke commending words that have gone down in history. (loc)

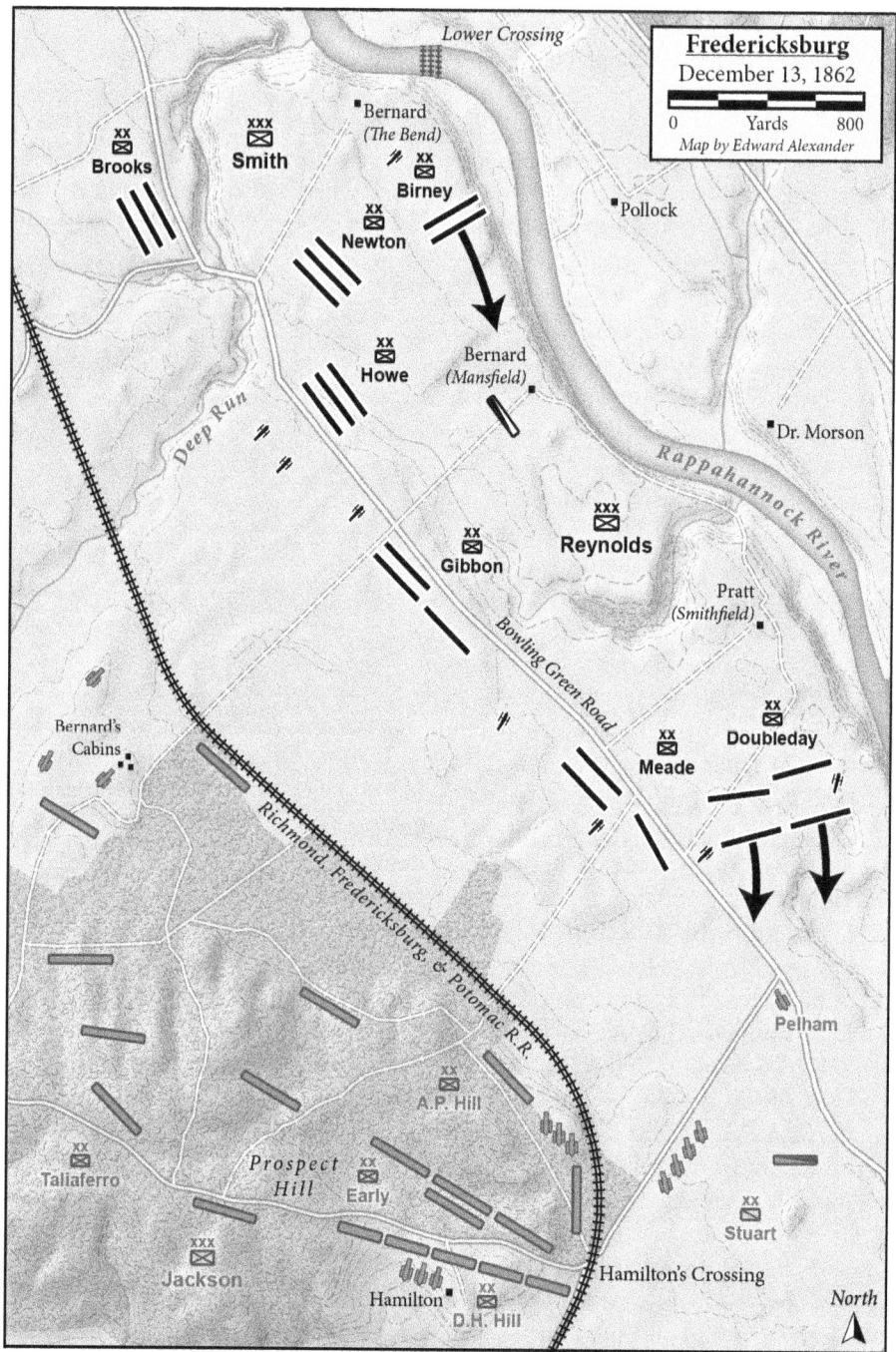

FREDERICKSBURG—On the morning of December 13, 1862, Pelham took a cannon to an advanced position and fired on the flank of Union infantry.

The open fields of Slaughter Pen Farm are preserved by the American Battlefield Trust. Pelham's advanced position was roughly a mile southeast of this location (left from this photo's perspective). (skb)

The morning of December 13, 1862, dawned with a ground fog laying over the open fields in Jackson's front. Union infantry formed lines of battle under the cover of their artillery on both sides of the river. The quiet anticipation hung in the sharp winter air. Too quiet, in Pelham's opinion. He asked Stuart for permission to take a single gun in advance of the Confederate line and fire on the Union infantry's flank. Stuart and Jackson agreed, and the cavalry general sent a message to Lee: "Jackson has not advanced, but I have, and I am going to crowd them with artillery." Pelham went looking for a cannon and crew to take on his morning escapade. British Captain Phillips offered Pelham a ribbon tie with the colors of his British regiment, asking him to wear it as a talisman and then return it to him after the action. Pelham acquiesced and rode on.

Although other cannoneers later claimed with disdain and admiration that Pelham took their gun, it is nearly certain that Pelham selected his favorite 12-pound Napoleon, gunners from the "Napoleon Detachment" of his original battery, and their current commander, Capt. Mathis W. Henry, to go out into the advanced position. Nearly a mile in advance of the Confederate line, Pelham carefully selected his terrain, using a ground depression and cedar hedge to partly conceal his position. About four hundred yards away, unsuspecting Union infantrymen waited, tensely focused on the open ground to their front, unaware of the deadly detachment positioning on their left flank. Pelham's first shot sent a solid cannonball arching through the morning air, opening the battle of Fredericksburg on that fateful day.

Alexander Bates in the 7th Pennsylvania Reserves described the moment of Pelham's opening shot:

These engraved words are on a stone marker placed in the post-war era by James P. Smith, a staff officer of "Stonewall" Jackson, to commemorate Confederate positions during battles in central Virginia. (skb)

When thus standing in line, a cannon boomed out on our left, at close range, seemingly on the Bowling Green road. A shot whizzed high in the air, passing over our heads from left to right along the line. Naturally supposing from our position, 'twas one of our own batteries. We thought our gunners had had a little too much "commissary" this morning, and so remarked. Another report, then a third, each time the missile coming lower in the air, when they discovered 'twas the enemy. The order was given "down" when from the force of the custom we fell forward face downward. I had no time to notice who remained standing being naturally engaged in pressing down hard, bearing on and flattening out that I might not interfere with any of the flying iron. This single gun, as subsequently learned, was commanded by Major John Pelham. . . . He soon got the range when his shells exploded low overhead and on the flanks of the regiments. The field officers of the Seventh were dismounted close in our rear. A large fragment of shell with force somewhat spent (I saw it fall) struck Adjutant Harvey's horse, tearing down a triangular piece of hide from its side which hung down some fifteen inches. The animal remained quietly in place as though it, too, deemed this part of the program. I could now see some of the happenings, for after Major Pelham had introduced himself, got range, &c., we suddenly became familiar with his manner, and were encouraged to a certain extent to raise our heads and look about while he amused himself.

Pelham's amusement did not last long without resistance. Battery A of the 1st Pennsylvania Light Artillery moved to open a counter fire, and Union guns from across the Rappahannock River also opened fire, trying to locate the position of Pelham's gun and assuming there was more artillery and possibly supporting infantry there, too. At least five Union batteries engaged Pelham's gun. Some projectiles stuck too close, killing or badly wounding a couple

Confederate gunners. One gunner fell as he sponge swabbed the cannon, barely able to speak, "Tell mother I die bravely," before he died.

As the unequal fight continued, Lee observed it and said he would have preferred Stuart to delay the battle's opening, but warmly praised Pelham's action, remarking on his gallantry. "It is glorious to see such courage in one so young!" Lee exclaimed as Pelham continued to maintain his advanced position and paralyzed the Union infantry for nearly an hour. The accolades from the commander of the Army of Northern Virginia sealed the artillery major's moniker as "Gallant Pelham" and were widely reported in newspaper accounts of the battle of Fredericksburg in the south, north, and Europe.

Stuart began to worry, sending messengers into the firestorm to check on Pelham and suggested that it was time to withdraw to the main Confederate line. One rider later claimed: "I had to take a message to Pelham from General Stuart during the hottest part of that fight. I had to run the gauntlet between the enemies batteries, and ours to find Pelham, and I found him way down next to the river. He was calmly sitting on his horse with one leg thrown over the pannell [pommel?] of his saddle giving orders. I rode up and delivered General Stuart's message, which was to ask him how he was getting on. His reply was, "Go back and tell General Stuart I am doing first rate; that I have only lost one man so far." Pelham had selected his position well. By shifting the exact location of the Napoleon between shots, he managed to keep the Union gunners uncertain and unable to place a direct hit. Stuart attempted to send a second cannon into the advanced position, but that reinforcement gun took a poor position and was quickly disabled. To other messengers, Pelham insisted he would stay until his ammunition ran out—a typical preference and tactic that Pelham employed during his advance escapades. Another messenger from Stuart carried the words: "Get back from destruction, you infernal, gallant fool, John Pelham!"

"Gallant Pelham"—the nickname most associated with the young Alabamian—stems from Lee's compliments to Pelham during the battle of Fredericksburg. (skb)

Finally, with his ammunition running low, having successfully delayed Union movements for around an hour, and drawing the intense fire of several enemy batteries, Pelham ordered his gunners to withdraw. The deed was done, observed, praised, and ready for legendary status. For his own part, Pelham routinely deflected praise to Capt. Henry.

Pelham's opening fight was the prelude to the rest of the battle of Fredericksburg on December 13. Union infantry assaulted Jackson's line and, finding a weak, unguarded place, broke through until a Confederate counterattack sent them reeling back. The battle then shifted to Marye's Heights as brigade after brigade assaulted that Confederate defensive position until darkness fell and dead and wounded men in blue carpeted the open ground.

A shopping center and several acres of Central Virginia Battlefield Trust's preserved land are called "Pelham's Corner," roughly the position that Pelham brought his single gun early on December 13. (skb)

Pelham took command of artillery on Jackson's flank, receiving 15 additional guns under his temporary command and setting up a crossfire cover with other Confederate artillery from Prospect Hill. The Stuart Horse Artillery engaged at a distance and took some casualties during the rest of the battle day. In the night after the battle, Pelham followed Jackson's orders to prepare for a counterattack and later quickly constructed defensive earthworks for the artillery. Satisfied with Pelham's heroics and skills, Jackson remarked to Stuart: "Have you another Pelham, General? If so, I wish you would give him to me."

Pvt. William P. Walters wrote to his wife a few days after the battle, describing the difficult day:

> *Our battery was in all day and our loss was severe. We had 2 men killed and 8 wounded. There were 3 Floyd boys wounded, Joseph Phlegar, Samuel Evans and Henderson Boothe. The other 5 all slightly wounded but 1 man lost his arm. . . . It was a hot fight. The cannons [opened] at daylight and went on till dark. Both sides stood their ground. We were under a shower of shells all day. Our loss was greater than all our loss before since last spring put together. Our company has been in many hard places but we always came out safe before, but we ought to be thankful that we come*

out. . . . for it looked to me like there were cannon balls enough shot at us to kill the whole army. . . . There isn't any fun in this sort of work, so I won't say any more about it. . . .

On December 19, Steven Dandridge, the son of the Adam Stephen Dandridge of "The Bower," wrote to his family, making mention of Pelham's teasing:

In the battle of Fredericksburg we lost 6 killed and ten or twelve badly wounded. Our camp is nothing like it used to be, a look of sorrow now sits upon the countenance of every one. . . . Oh! How thankful we ought to be to that God who has so mercifully protected us. . . . Tell Sal [Sallie] that Pelham had command of us in the fight. He said that he would keep us in until I got killed and then he would relieve our company. He is as gallant a fellow as I ever saw.

The Confederate victory at Fredericksburg finished a year of successes in the east. In most actions and countless unnamed skirmishes, Pelham and his horse artillery had contributed to the Confederate successes. They had gone from an unknown battery to an artillery command with five batteries and numerous mentions for bravery. Pelham had started the year as Stuart's artillery protégé and ended as a household name for those following Confederate battlefield achievements and victories. Despite the dangerous odds, Pelham survived 1862 without major injury. Did he feel invincible? Did time seem to be running out? Or had he so calmly settled that pain or death could find him at any time that he lived with a reckless, glorious courage?

The Central Virginia Battlefield Trust preserved and maintains several acres at Pelham's Corner. In recent years, they have been planting cedar trees/bushes as a nod to the description of bushes that helped to hide Pelham's gun from Union artillerists. (skb)

Winter:
"Ever up with the cavalry"

CHAPTER THIRTEEN

The fighting paused. They gathered the wounded, buried the dead in the freezing ground, and created winter camps. What did Pelham think? How did he reflect on the record of his year? What did he tell his family? Did he live in hope or have no time to be young in a world growing old with war? Then Christmas came. Like the previous seven Christmases, Pelham was far from home.

On December 25, John Pelham attended a Christmas dinner at "Stonewall" Jackson's headquarters at Moss Neck Planation, south of Fredericksburg, in Caroline County. The feast included a turkey, homemade foods sent in food boxes from the Shenandoah Valley, and oysters gathered from Port Royal. Generals Lee, Stuart, Pendleton, Maj. Pelham, and "numerous staff" gathered for a cheerful dinner party in a large tent.

Stuart celebrated, but did not remain idle for long. On December 26, with selected men including Pelham and some of the horse artillery, he set off on the Dumfries Raid, striking into northern Virginia,

Winter 1862–1863 had calm and adventure for the Confederate cavalry and horse artillery even as freezing weather and snow presented challenges for feeding horses and men. (skb)

The Fairfax Raid gave some snowy, winter experiences to Pelham and the Stuart Horse Artillery. (skb)

near Washington City to capture supplies and startle the Federals. The raid did not go completely according to plan, but by January 1, 1863, the riders returned to their winter camp, and Stuart was still pleased with the exploit. They had captured approximately 250 prisoners, a couple hundred horses and mules, and twenty wagons of small arms and ammunition with the loss of one Confederate killed, 13 wounded and 14 missing. As usual, Stuart praised Pelham in his report, noting, "his horse artillery, performed gallant and exceedingly difficult service during this expedition. Ever up with the cavalry, he crossed the Occoquan at Selectman's Ford, which has always been considered impracticable for vehicles."

Back in camp, Pelham settled into a routine and leadership for his stationary batteries. Officers spent part of that winter writing belated battle reports; some—especially "Stonewall" Jackson—were woefully behind in their summaries. On January 10, Jedediah Hotchkiss, Jackson's chief topographical engineer and mapmaker, consulted with Pelham about the battle of Groveton (Second Manassas). This meeting prompted Pelham to write the observations which formed his "report" of that battle which eventually went into the Official Records after the war.

Throughout the winter weeks, Pelham often appeared as a welcomed guest at the dining tables of fellow officers and civilians. On January 16, Capt. Charles M. Blackford wrote, "William and Majors von Borcke, Fitzhugh, and Pelham dined with me last night." A civilian girl who lived at Hayfield, a home about ten miles south of Fredericksburg along the Rappahannock River, later recalled:

We would often seen the generals. On one occasion Generals Lee, Jackson, Stuart, Pendleton and Major John Pelham from Alabama (The Gallant Pelham, General Lee called him) were all in the dining room at Hayfield at one time. General Lee looked over at Major Pelham who was sitting by a window and said, "There sits Major Pelham looking today as if butter wouldn't melt in his mouth, but in battle he is a perfect lion. The reason he looks so modest today is he has on a borrowed overcoat." With that the blood mounted in Major Pelham's face up to his forehead, and when he got up to leave the overcoat almost touched the floor. He walked close to the wall so it wouldn't be noticed. He was so young and brave. Just a beautiful boy.

Heros von Borcke, a Prussian, served on Stuart's staff and seems to have been one of Pelham's friends. Many fond and colorful stories appear in von Borcke's memoirs, and his diary is a useful resource for learning about Pelham's whereabouts during the winter. (loc)

In mid-January, Stuart sent Pelham and von Borcke to Culpeper Court House to prepare for a cavalry review. Confederate cavalry covered a wide territory along the Rappahannock River, and officers often journeyed between camps to handle discipline, supplies, and other matters. Later that week, Stuart decided to leave Pelham and von Borcke in Culpeper to finish cavalry business. The two friends took residence at the Virginia Hotel and formed an acquaintance with the family living in the fine home across the street. Judge Henry Shackelford and his daughters, though originally Unionist in their preferences, offered hospitality, and Pelham and von Borcke spent their spare time constructing a board walk across the muddy quagmire so they could visit in the evenings without bringing excessive amounts of Virginia mud into the house. One of the young women—Bessie Shackelford—later remembered Pelham fondly, remarking on his good humor, dancing skills, and quiet conversation. With business complete in Culpeper, the two officers returned to the cavalry camp near Fredericksburg, leaving behind their acquaintances but with invitations to visit again.

Pelham also made a visit or two to Richmond on military business, meeting with ordinance officers about ammunition for his batteries. He may have got

Quiet, snow-filled Virginia woods were likely a familiar sight to Pelham as he rode across central Virginia counties, checking on artillery camps or following Stuart's orders. (skb)

into some type of social trouble or escapade during a Richmond trip; a mysterious note from John E. Cooke to a female relative directed her to not believe all the rumors she had heard about Pelham's recent trip to the Confederate capital.

Pelham exhibited some excitement about a new artillery addition to his command. A 6-pound Whitworth gun arrived from Europe through the blockade, and Pelham received orders to assign it to the special command of an artillery lieutenant. He selected Lt. William Hoxton, the brother of a West Point classmate, though the incident prompted a letter from Pelham describing his commitment to promotions by merit and not friendships. "As soon as I got full command of my company I strangled the great enemy to our Service[:] 'popular election' of officers, and had men promoted for distinguished gallantry."

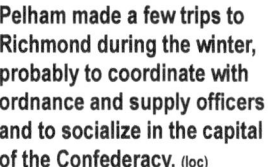

Pelham made a few trips to Richmond during the winter, probably to coordinate with ordnance and supply officers and to socialize in the capital of the Confederacy. (loc)

However, all of Pelham's good intentions could not solve the supply problems. In the cavalry camps from Culpeper to Caroline County, horses suffered and died from lack of forage and disease. Keeping regular rations for the men also proved challenging. Though in surviving letters to fellow officers, Pelham maintained a positive outlook and an anxious hope for the next raid or campaign.

Stuart and other generals advocated again for Pelham's promotion. By February 5, Custis Lee wrote to Stuart: "In reference to Pelham, I should think from your statement that there would be no difficulty about his promotion." Still, the official steps for that new rank delayed in Richmond, prompting Stuart to complain that they were purposely neglectful because of Pelham's age and appeal to President Davis.

The calendar turned to March. On the 8th, Pelham visited friends from Alabama and received a unique gift—a cannonball—from a young woman in his home state. He penned a thank you note to "Miss Moore" and a draft of his letter still exists: "I visited

This building is the refurbished and refronted hotel where Pelham and Von Borcke stayed in Culpeper. The now-paved street would have been the muddy mess that they "bridged" to visit the Shackelford's Home without tracking mud into the parlor. (skb)

This photograph shows a Whitworth cannon that Union troops captured. In the winter of 1863, Pelham was excited to receive a Whitworth gun and experiment with the British gift. (loc)

Col O'Neal and Sam yesterday. The latter handed me your note and the cannon ball. . . . Permit me to express my sincerest thanks, both for your kind note and the confidence you show in entrusting the projectile to my care. I promise faithfully it shall be returned to its former owners with all the bitterness and force you could desire and with all the accuracy my limited experience will permit. Nor shall it be carelessly thrown away. I will reserve it till we get to 'close quarters'—and then one prayer for Alabama and yourself. You must grant me permission to make an official report to you of the success or non-success of the shot. I hope and believe it cannot fail. I am proud of the honor you do me in allowing me to fire it for you." The cannonball's fate was not recorded.

Military duties pulled Pelham from camp in the following week. In a seemingly odd series of events, Pelham snuck out of camp with an unofficial furlough on March 15, though officially heading to Orange Court House with the reason of inspecting Moorman's Battery. Annoyed at Pelham's departure, Stuart sent a messenger, ordering him to come back. The major continued to Orange Court House and obey Stuart's order the next day instead of turning back immediately and riding in the dark. For some reason, Pelham wanted to get to Orange Court House; he spent part of that evening in the company of several young women, including Nannie Price and someone known only as Miss Brill. If there was another young woman there with a stronger connection or interest to Pelham, her name has escaped history thus far.

The next morning—March 16—word reached Orange Court House that a Union cavalry movement seemed to be underway closer to Culpeper Court House. Pelham decided to go there; perhaps he had also heard that Stuart headed to Culpeper to participate in a court martial, and he could most quickly rejoin with Stuart there. By late afternoon, Pelham arrived in Culpeper and heard reports about Confederate cavalry eyeing a Union movement near Kelly's Ford, a few miles northeast of the county seat. Satisfied with the precautions Gen. Fitz Lee had taken, Stuart and Pelham remained in Culpeper for the evening.

A major's star was embroidered on red facings (for artillery) on this Confederate officer's uniform. As far as is known today, none of Pelham's uniforms have survived. (skb)

In later years, various writers placed Pelham at several places throughout the evening of March 16: visiting the Shackelford home, chatting with a gathering of officers in a room of the Virginia Hotel, or lodging for the night at Redwood, a home outside of town belonging to distant relatives of the Dandridge's from "The Bower." He may have visited all locations as the evening hours ticked by.

In the darkness beyond the light of the rooms in Culpeper, Union cavalry readied along the Rappahannock River. A new Union commander for the Army of the Potomac—Maj. Gen. Joseph Hooker—planned to use cavalry in his strategies. The blue-clad troopers wanted to conduct their own raids, and with growing skill and confidence rising, they prepared to challenge the prowess of the Confederate cavalry. Underneath the enjoyable moments and military business of winter, Pelham longed to return to combat. He anticipated the opening of spring fighting. He had written to a friend, "I hope "Fighting Joe" Hooker will come over and give us a chance as soon as the weather will permit. This army is invincible—whenever you hear of it fighting you may add one more name to our list of victories for will certainly be the result."

Kelly's Ford:
"Bleeding profusely"

CHAPTER FOURTEEN

A messenger brought the news to the Confederate officers in Culpeper on March 17, 1863. Yankees attempted to cross at Kelly's Ford on the Rappahannock River, about 12 miles by road northeast of the town. The news disrupted Pelham's morning, whether it woke him, merely hurried his preparations for the day, or interrupted his breakfast. At some point, he jotted a brief note to Capt. Moorman, whose artillery battery waited at Orange Court House, apprising the officer of the situation as he understood it at that moment and making plans for the following day.

Culpeper, C.H.
March 17, 1863

Capt.
Be on the alert. Large force of cavalry between Morrisville and Bealton Station. If everything is quiet here I will be at Rapidann Station tomorrow.

Mo.[st] Respty[Respectfully],
Jno. Pelham, Maj. Art.[illery]

Looking north along the Rappahannock River from the vicinity of Kelly's Ford. Upriver from the actual ford, most of the battle of Kelly's Ford unfolded on March 17, 1863. (skb)

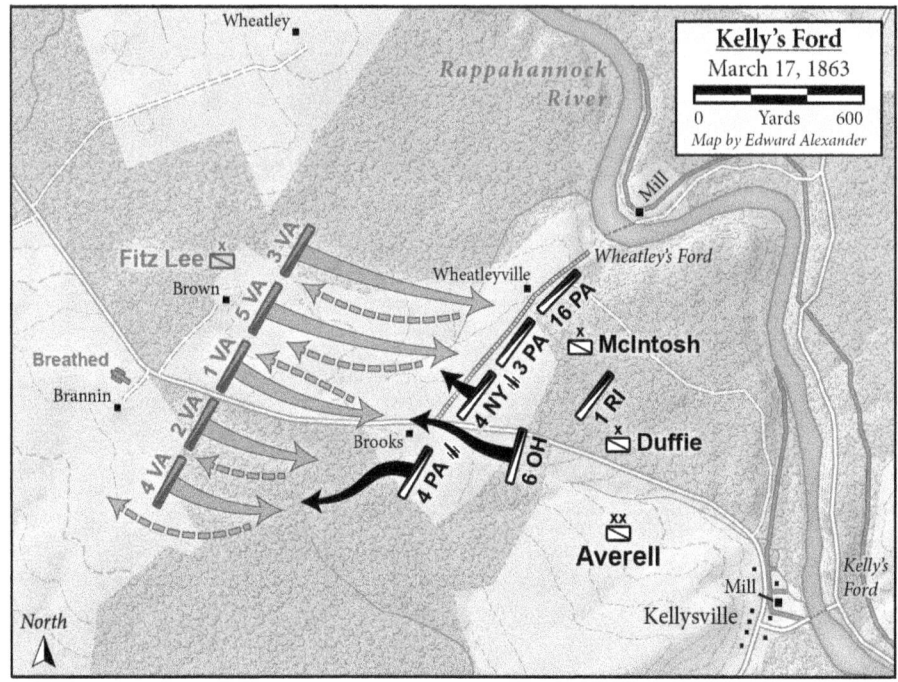

KELLY'S FORD—At Kelly's Ford, Union cavalry took position behind a stone wall, letting Confederates charge toward them while artillery on both sides fired into the cavalry confusion.

General Fitzhugh Lee commanded Confederate cavalry at Kelly's Ford and during the battle. Though Stuart came to view the battle, he left Lee in command, only offering assistance or support as needed or requested. (loc)

Stuart decided to ride toward Kelly's Ford and see how Gen. Fitzhugh Lee managed the battle and provide aid if necessary. Joining Stuart, Pelham rode down Main Street, heading toward the distant fight. Bessie Shackelford at the window or on the porch of her family's home, waving her handkerchief to the passing officers. Outside Culpeper, patches of snow whitened the landscape , and the roads to Kelly's Ford were icy mud that morning. A brisk wind cut through Central Virginia, but the "bright and clear" day offered good viewing for a cavalry fight.

Pelham headed toward a battle that had started around daybreak, and he arrived at the battlefield around mid to late morning. Union Gen. William Averell, with approximately 2,100 cavalrymen, had braved the freezing rain of the previous day to maneuver toward Culpeper Court House and threaten the Confederate camps and communication lines. Confederate Gen. Fitzhugh Lee had strengthened the number of cavalry pickets along the river, and around daybreak on March 17, gunfire erupted at Kelly's Ford. The battle raged across the river, but eventually

Union troopers crossed the ford, driving back the 800 engaged Confederates for a couple of miles.

Stuart and Pelham observed that the fighting shifted from the river to the open fields and patchy pine woods. While some Union troopers dismounted and used a large stone wall for shelter, more cavalrymen joined the line and would take part in the fighting that marked a turning point of Union cavalry taking the field with confidence against the mostly undefeated Confederate horsemen. Subsequent phases of the battle involved Confederate regimental charges against the Union position at the stonewall.

Pelham began looking for artillery opportunities. He knew that Capt. James Breathed's cannoneers were encamped about three-and-a-half miles away and hurrying to the battle. Pelham had good instincts for placing a battery effectively and studied the topography. The battlefield was comparatively flat, and the hamlet of Kellysville and several farms—notably the Brannin's, Brown's, and Wheatley's—lay in the path of the advancing Union force. Pelham chose Brannin House for the initial artillery position for Capt. Breathed's guns; this would place the four cannons near the Federals' left flank as they anchored and readied at the prominent stonewall.

Artillerist Pvt. H. H. Matthews remembered the hurried advance: "The horses were in a run and as the road was very slippery owning to the recent snow having melted, it made traveling at our pace very dangerous. Still we went on until we came to the line of our brigade near the Brannon House, where we were ordered into position." Pelham joined with Breathed, offering suggestions and watching the Blakely cannons begin to engage the Union artillery. Pelham ordered: "Captain, do not let your fire cease; drive them from their position." Throughout the remainder of the battle, the Confederate cannons dueled with the Union guns at a distance of about 3,000 yards. Matthews declared, "We had a battle royal holding our own."

Cavalry officer Henry Gilmor described the unfolding scene: "The fighting became general, and every regiment of ours might be seen in different parts of the field charging the enemy's advancing columns and lines, driving them back on their strong reserves,

General William Averell led Union cavalry across the river, advanced from Kelly's Ford, and took a defensive position near a stonewall. Some historians see the battle of Kelly's Ford as a turning point and the beginning of the successful rise of Union cavalry in the east—a credible force and threat to Confederate cavalry and Confederate escapades. (loc)

Henry Gilmor wrote memoirs about his cavalry experiences of the Civil War. While he was prone to exaggeration, many of his details about Pelham's death corroborate other eyewitness accounts. (loc)

Snow still lay on the ground as the battle of Kelly's Ford was fought, creating a slushy, frozen mess. (skb)

The John Pelham Historical Association placed this memorial between the old stone wall and the Rappahannock River at the heart of Kelly's Ford battlefield. Whether Pelham charged this far forward remains a point for study. (skb)

and then falling back to reform and charge again." Cavalrymen of both sides claimed to have fought brutally with sabers at Kelly's Ford and engaged in hand-to-hand combat.

Pelham may have ridden toward the stonewall in one of the Confederate regimental charges. His name is sometimes associated with the charge of the 3rd Virginia. For example, Stuart's staff officer Henry B. McClellan claimed, "He [Pelham] rode forward to aid in leading the charge of the 3d regiment. . . ." Heros Von Borcke who was not an eyewitness to the battle claimed that "When one of our regiments advancing to charge was received with such a terrible fire by the enemy as to cause it to waver, Pelham galloped up to them, shouting, 'Forward, boys! forward to victory and glory!'" In the historiography of Kelly's Ford, survivors amended their original versions to include Pelham riding in a cavalry charge based on non-eyewitness accounts. Pelham may have rallied cavalry regiments for their charges but stayed behind or returned to Breathed's guns. Eyewitness Henry Gilmor placed him there in his initial writings about the battle.

Pelham and Gilmor watched the fight near the 2nd Virginia Cavalry's position and near Breathed's guns. A shell from a Union gun exploded nearby. Pelham did not relocate. It was just another shell on another battlefield, seeking another breathing target. General Fitzhugh Lee rode along the line, while the cavalrymen cheered him. Union artillery continued to target the cavalry regiment and officers riding the line. Nearby, a horse was shot, and Pelham paused his own horse, making suggestions for the wounded animal's treatment. A deafening explosion rocked the

scene. Pieces of an artillery shell rained down. The man with the wounded horse looked up to ask Pelham a question. All he saw was an empty saddle.

"My God, they've killed poor Pelham!" someone screeched above the battle's noise. Henry Gilmor turned. Pelham's riderless horse was ambling away, and "Pelham himself [was] lying on his back upon the ground, his eyes wide open, and looking very natural, but fatally hurt." At that moment, Pelham crashed into passivity, no longer active in the final hours of his life. The rest of his mortal life and his place in historical memory rested in others' hands.

Adding to Gilmor's dismay, the cavalry skirmish lines shifted ever closer. With assistance from two other officers, Gilmor placed Pelham's body in front of his saddle and rode to a safer place. Gently, he examined, finding that Pelham "had been struck on the back of the head, and was bleeding profusely." Gilmor transferred Pelham's limp body to another horse and ordered two dismounted cavalrymen to take him to an ambulance and get a surgeon.

Believing that Pelham was dead, Gilmor galloped back into the battle to find Gen. Stuart. He found the general nearly "cut off from our own troops by a sudden advance of a strong body of the enemy." When Stuart saw Pelham's blood splattered on the officer's uniform and heard the news about his artillerist, an expression of "distress and horror" passed over his face. Halting briefly in a dense wood, Stuart asked Gilmor to repeat the particulars. "Then he bowed his head upon his horse's neck. 'Our loss is irreparable!' he exclaimed."

Kelly's Ford is located downriver from the modern road and bridge. Union cavalrymen splashed across the icy-cold river here in the dark, early hours of March 17, 1863. The ford is noticeable when the water runs low, particularly in the summer—like this photo. (skb)

$\mathcal{D}eath:$
"$\mathcal{W}ithout\ a\ struggle$"

CHAPTER FIFTEEN

His legs hung on one side of the horse and his head and arms trailed down the other side. Pelham's attendants strolled toward Brandy Station, leading the horse with the bloody body. The cavalrymen had not located an ambulance, and they had not found a surgeon. Perhaps they thought this officer was dead and their easy way to escape the battlefield.

John Pelham was still alive. However, draped over a horse, with blood rushing to his head and the site of his injury, he gave no signs of life to those who were not looking. He seems to have been silent, probably unconscious. The method of transportation doing nothing to help his chances of recovery and quite possibly sealing his fate.

Henry Gilmor rode toward Culpeper through Brandy Station, carrying a message to the telegraph for Stuart. Four miles down the road, he came upon the slow-moving soldiers, horse, and wounded Pelham. Furious at the lack of care and disobedience to his orders, Gilmor re-examined Pelham and confirmed that he still breathed. He pulled the major

The Virginia State Capitol as it appears in the early 21st century. Pelham's body lay in state in the historic portion of this building. (skb)

An ambulance—perhaps similar to the one that eventually transported Pelham—was a quick but uncomfortable experience for wounded soldiers. (loc)

off the horse, laid him flat on the ground, and sent orders for an ambulance. Private Joseph Minghini, a temporary courier assisting Stuart that day, found Pelham around this time and oversaw the next stage of his transportation.

In Gilmor's opinion, "I firmly believe that, had surgical aid been called to the remove the compression on the brain, his life might have been saved." But time had passed, and pressure had almost certainly increased within Pelham's skull while he hung upside down and bleeding. Gilmor noted that Pelham's "face, hair, and hands were caked and clotted with mud and blood."

Someone finally found an ambulance, and Pelham was placed inside the medical wagon to complete the journey to Culpeper. He was one of the approximately 211 total casualties of the battle of Kelly's Ford. The fight raged as Union troopers continued to drive the Confederates back, marking the first significant stand-up cavalry fight in the eastern theater. However, by afternoon, Averell had had enough and wanted his men to know their success. He made a tactical withdrawal from the field and recrossed the Rappahannock River, allowing the Confederates to repossess the ford and keep their communication lines to Culpeper.

The ambulance with Pelham's unconscious form rolled up the incline of Culpeper's Main Street and stopped at Henry Shackelford's home. Someone carried him into the house, through the doorway and passed the parlor where he had spent pleasant winter hours in civilian company. Military surgeons arrived, and Dr. Herndon, a local medical man, "was sent for to see him & everything was done for him that could be."

The Shackelford women "had all things in readiness for his reception." They may have assisted in cleaning away the blood and battlefield mud from their young patient. "After, by gentle hands, he had been washed with warm water, his feet and hands swathed in flannel, and some brandy poured into his mouth, the surgeons commenced relieve the compression on the brain."

The doctors extracted a shell fragment, discovering that Pelham's skull "was badly shattered" in the two inches "between the entrance and exit" but

that his brain had not been pierced. They removed pieces of bone from the injury and consulted. A skull fracture—particularly if the brain had not been hit—was not an immediate death sentence in Civil War era medicine; pages of cases recorded in the Surgical Record of the War of the Rebellion detail wounds like Pelham's, where the patient made a full recovery. However, the injury, brain pressure, or swelling during part of his evacuation, and the blood rush to his head had created compounding difficulties. Three doctors said Pelham's recovery was hopeless and left him to the comfort care of his friends.

The Shackelford Home no longer stands, but this photograph shows its appearance. (cl)

Shadows lengthened as March 17, and the battle of Kelly's Ford ended. Military men and civilian friends in Culpeper slipped into the Shackelford home to inquire about Pelham or see him lying comfortable and unconscious. Darkness came, midnight passed, and Pelham still breathed.

This plaque is fixed on a modern structure in Culpeper, Virginia, at the site of the Shackelford Home and the site of Pelham's death on March 18, 1863. (skb)

John Pelham had lived 24 years. He had run wild with his brothers in Alabama before settling to responsibility on his farm. He had learned military discipline, duties, and academics at West Point. He had made a choice to fight for the Confederacy. Pelham felt his beliefs about war shifted from "glorious" to heart sickening. Yet he built, trained, and led one of the famed fighting units within the Army of Northern Virginia: the Stuart Horse Artillery. On rises of high ground from the Virginia Peninsula to Nicodemus Heights and Fredericksburg and dozens of unnamed places in between, he had positioned cannons and aimed with deadly precision. He had seen his name rise to notable status within the Confederacy and internationally. Fame had made him uncomfortable. He seemed most at ease in the "heat and flush of battle," or perhaps with his closest friends, who understood the thoughts and hopes that he kept from public display. He had plans for the future as he had ridden toward Kelly's Ford. Twenty-four years was all he had, before the day an artillery shell fragment pierced his skull and laid him senseless at the threshold of death and eternity. Gilmor recalled: "About one [A.M.] his eyes opened—he turned toward [me with] an unconscious look—then closed them—drew a long breath, and died without a struggle."

Realizing their friend was gone, Henry Gilmor and Bessie Shackelford prepared Pelham's body. They had just completed

Following Pelham's death, the Stuart Horse Artillery and Confederate cavalry mourned Pelham by Stuart's order. Later, Robert F. Beckham took command of the Stuart Horse Artillery, followed later by James Breathed. (skb)

their sorrowful task when "the door was gently opened, and Stuart entered." Stuart's grief—though deeply personal—marked the beginning of others coming to grips with the loss of Pelham. Over the next hours, days, and years, various meanings would become attached to Pelham's life, death, and memory. Born out of a genuine desire to honor and remember, the memorialization of the young artillerist's life would eventually reach legendary proportions.

The construction of Pelham's place in Confederate memory began on March 18, when Gen. Stuart shifted his personal grief to the national scene. Staff officer Heros von Borcke received a telegram from Stuart that morning, instructing him to go to Hanover Junction and prepare to meet the train that would carry Pelham's body to Richmond. Von Borcke would oversee the funerals and then return Pelham's remains to his remains to his parents in Alabama. As von Borcke made ready for the journey, news of Pelham's death spread through the main cavalry camp.

It would take longer for the tragic announcement to reach Dr. and Mrs. Pelham in Alabama. However, two individuals who had known Pelham probably longer than anyone else in Virginia were confronted with grief and confusion. Willis and Newton—the enslaved men whom Pelham had brought to war with him—approached von Borcke "with tokens of great distress" and "begged to be allowed to go and take charge of their master's body—a permission which I was, however, constrained to refuse." Pelham's funeral in Richmond would be a public affair, handled by white men. Willis and Newton were not allowed to travel back to Alabama with Pelham's body. They were eventually returned to Dr. Pelham with the shipment of possessions: "his trunk . . . his sabre, two servants, and two horses," a solemn reminder of the Confederacy's view of "camp servants."

When von Borcke arrived at Hanover Junction, he found Pelham's wooden casket and telegrammed to Richmond to begin preparations. Arriving in the Confederate capital, he contacted Virginia Governor Letcher, Alabama congressmen, and politicians who knew the Pelham Family. Together, they decided that Pelham's body should lie in state in the Virginia State Capitol building and after 36 hours begin a railroad journey with a military escort to his home state. By the night of March 18, Pelham's wooden coffin rested in the capitol building, draped with a Virginia state flag, and watched by an honor guard.

A train took Pelham's remains from Culpeper to Gordonsville to Richmond . . . and eventually over other railroad tracks to Alabama. (loc)

An unidentified woman wearing a mourning dress and photographed at Lookout Mountain. Unverifiable rumors claim that several young women wore mourning for Pelham; women also wore mourning for other fallen Confederate leaders as a sign of sorrow and respect. (loc)

Pelham's body lay in state under the marbled eyes of a statue of George Washington. (skb)

Von Borcke spared no effort in his preparations to both honor and safeguard Pelham's body. On the morning of March 19, he procured a "handsome iron coffin," and "by special request . . . had a small glass window let into the coffin lid just over the face, that his friends and admirers might take a last look at the young hero."

For 36 hours, Major Pelham's remains lay beneath the marbled gaze of George Washington in the center rotunda of the Virginia state capitol. His battlefield victories in Virginia had secured him—in death—a place in the Old Dominion's adoptive legends. Nor was it merely a symbolic honor. Hundreds, possibly thousands, of Virginians and others living in the Confederate capital filed past the casket to pay their respects.

An anonymous writer known as "Evelyn" described the scene:

> *I have just returned from the Capitol, and with saddened spirit sit down and write of the dear dead boy now lying there—Alabama's noblest tribute of the whole war. His coffin stands in the hall, upon a pedestal arranged for the purpose. A sentinel passes backwards and forwards beside it. Upon the top are*

the flags he fought so bravely to sustain; and upon them a mourning wreath of evergreens. Beside it—just over the manly heart, no still forever—lies a single snow-white flower. . . .

In a scene similar to the one that would be repeated after "Stonewall" Jackson's death six weeks later, women "brought garlands and magnificent bouquets to lay on the coffin." The public grief extended to wearing mourning badges, and according to oft-repeated stories, several young women wore full mourning.

On March 20, at 5:00 p.m., von Borcke oversaw the removal of Pelham's coffin from the capitol. A convalescent Alabama soldier who knew the Pelham family served as the official escort for the trip. Serving as an honor guard, the Richmond Battalion of Infantry led the way to the train station. The mournful Dead March echoed along the street as "gallant Pelham" started his final journey home. Nearly two years before, John Pelham had reportedly told his mother, "Your boy wants to come back" but also indicated that he recognized that he could be taken "safe from the battlefield" by death. Martha Pelham waited in Alabama; her son was returning to her in a casket.

Mourning and mourning ritual was important in Civil War America, creating layers of memory. Pelham's funerals included religious, military, and cultural rituals. (loc)

Memory:
"His is the glory of duty done!"

CHAPTER SIXTEEN

A hearse waited at the remote train depot called Blue Mountain to take Pelham's body on the last part of his journey to his waiting family. Between March 20-28, the funeral procession had crossed four states, proceeded on nine different railroads and a steamboat, with a stop on March 26 at the state capitol building in Montgomery. There, Pelham's body lay in state at the direction of Governor John G. Shorter while hundreds of citizens passed the coffin. Finally, around 10:00 p.m. on March 28, under a full moon, the hearse rolled the last seven miles toward the Pelham family home. Local civilians surrounded the coffin, old men flanking it and young women following in procession. For a brief time, the Confederacy would give the officer back to his family.

Martha Pelham waited. "The Father and Sister were crushed and in sorrow kept their rooms," a relative recalled, "but that Spartan Mother met her beloved dead on the threshold as she would have done had been living and led the way into the parlor and directed where he must be laid where the light would

John Pelham's grave is in Jacksonville, Alabama. His parents and some of his siblings are buried nearby. (skb)

The Baptist Church in Jacksonville was the largest church in the community, and Pelham's funeral was held there, even though his family regularly attended the Presbyterian church. (skb)

fall on his face when Sunday [morning] came." The next day hundreds of people came to the home to pay their last respects. Meanwhile, friends and prominent community members formed a committee to arrange Pelham's last funeral and took the burden of those arrangements from the family.

On March 31, the funeral was held in Jacksonville, Alabama. So many people attended that the service had to be moved from the family's Presbyterian church to the larger Baptist church. Following the religious ceremony, Pelham's body was interred at the family plot in the Jacksonville town cemetery. In time, a 10-foot-tall marble column with a statue of "Gallant Pelham" was placed at his burial place.

As the Pelham family struggled to bear their grief, Confederate officers in Virginia continued their personal and ritual mourning. General Stuart issued General Orders No. 9 announcing Pelham's death to the army and reflecting on his military record: "His eye glanced over every battlefield of this army from the first Manassas to the moment of his death. . . .

Pelham's grave is maintained and regularly visited as people honor or wonder about his life and legacy. (skb)

This monument to Pelham has changed locations several times over the years. It now sits across from the Graffiti House at Brandy Station, Virginia, and is owned by a United Daughters of the Confederacy chapter in Alabama. The large stone beneath the marble pillar was taken from the stonewall at Kelly's Ford battlefield. (skb)

The memory of 'the gallant Pelham,' his many manly virtues, his noble nature and purity of character, are enshrined as a sacred legacy in the hearts of all who knew him." (Stuart eventually appointed Maj. Robert F. Beckham to command the Stuart Horse Artillery.) Stuart took time to write to Dr. Pelham, describing Maj. Pelham "as a brother" and asking the father to "permit me to share with you a grief so sacred, so consoling." In a letter to his wife, Stuart asked to name their next child John Pelham Stuart. When the baby was born, it was a girl, and they named her Virginia Pelham Stuart.

Downward crossed swords (or sabers) ornament another panel of the memorial at Pelham's grave, a reminder of his artillery leadership with Stuart's cavalry. (skb)

General Robert E. Lee, who had called Pelham "gallant" at Fredericksburg, offered private thoughts about the officer's death. "But I grieve over our noble dead! I do not know how I can replace the gallant Pelham. So young so true so brave. Though stricken down in the dawn of manhood, his is the glory of duty done!"

Other friends, officers, and soldiers wrote memorials about Pelham for publication or privately. Newspapers across the South and North carried the news of Pelham's death. Like during his bright moment

of fame after Fredericksburg, the *London Times* also reported his name and fall, describing Pelham as "one of the purest and bravest spirits which have yet been yielded up in this desolating war."

Pelham's death acquired meaning far beyond the personal grief of his family, his commander, and his comrades. The Confederacy had already been lionizing some of its fallen officers, but Pelham's war record, the national grief, and heroic-martyr status soared to new heights.

As the weeks, months, and years passed, the memory of John Pelham became less constrained by fact as he filled the Confederacy's need for a mythical hero and southern ideal. The man became marble, carved and molded to fit the perfections required of a selfless, sacrificial officer who dashed into combat and returned with victory, whose bachelor status allowed him to woo many girls, and who seemed to accept death as his fate in the service of the Confederacy.

Pelham was buried here in the spring of 1863. Years after the war ended, this memorial was erected. (skb)

Following the Confederacy's defeat in 1865, many southern men and women needed to give meaning to the losses they had endured and continue to justify their loss, sacrifices, and secession. An ideology known as the Lost Cause emerged. Part of the Lost Cause included the remembrance and veneration of Confederate officers. While Lee, Jackson, and Stuart were enduring favorites, John Pelham became one of the vaunted young officers to the Lost Cause adherents. Through family remembrances and the adoption of Pelham as a favored fallen hero by Confederate Veterans and the United Daughters of the Confederacy, he did not slip into obscurity.

The price for Pelham's fame within Confederate memory came at a cost. His war letters disappeared from his family's care, either lost, destroyed, or otherwise redacted during an early 20th-century research effort by a commander of the Confederate Veterans. The private and unknown moments of his life or relationships were filled in with fiction that matched the ideals needed in Confederate memory.

By the 1950s, Pelham's life had been conformed to the image of a young Lost Cause officer. Biographers over the decades perpetuated myths over reality, citing each other and continuing to fill in the blanks with speculations and implications.

Even in life, Pelham puzzled his friends. They struggled to reconcile the disparate stories with the man they knew. Bessie Shackelford of Culpeper offered one of the most thoughtful explanations of the juxtapositions of Pelham's character:

A boy, and yet a man, that was Pelham. You couldn't help being drawn to him . . . Sometimes I used to sit and just look at him and wonder if it could be true that he was the man they were all talking about, the man who could aim those guns so that they would kill and kill and kill. He didn't look as though he could ever order anybody to be killed. There wasn't a single line of hardness in his face. It was all tenderness and softness, as fresh and delicate as a boy's who liked people and who found the world good. I used to say to myself, 'A man like that—this boy?' That is really what he was, you know—a boy, a splendid boy.

Pelham's monument at Kelly's Ford battlefield can be challenging to find but frequently is found with unique memorial offerings by those who remember or admire his memory. (skb)

John Pelham's name has endured through memorialization efforts. However, seeing and understanding the young man without the exaggeration, molded perspectives, and suffocating agenda is challenging. At the heart of it all lies the truth; that Pelham was a remarkable young man who made difficult choices and followed his principles, displaying "glorious courage" on many of Virginia's battlefields from July 1861 through March 1863.

Many stories circulate in Civil War memory about John Pelham and his relationships. (skb)

John Pelham and the Girls

APPENDIX A

Author's Note: A confusing collection of stories have been associated with John Pelham's romantic interests, particularly during the Civil War years. Instead of accepting primary source hints as facts in the chapters of this biography, this appendix addresses the stories about the girls and women connected to Pelham's life in the historical context and record.

John Pelham died as a bachelor, and as time passed, this became part of the Lost Cause fascination with the 24-year-old artillery officer. Over the decades, biographers have taken advantage of the lack of conclusive information about Pelham's romantic life and drawn conclusions that reflect the culture of the era that the historiography was written. He has been portrayed as perfectly pure, implied to have been a womanizer, and hinted that he romantically preferred men. The lack of Pelham's letters and contradictory family memories adds to the confusion, and to some extent, the Lost Cause has victimized Pelham and his possible love interests, twisting vague hints to fit a culturally acceptable preference for this bachelor Confederate officer. What can be pieced together about romance and Pelham's life? And why did the Lost Cause take a vivid interest in this aspect of his private affairs?

Among the first women and girls that Pelham interacted with—though not in the romantic sense—were his mother, sister, cousins, and the enslaved females living at the family house and farms. Surviving letters suggest that Pelham had a close relationship with his mother and an affectionate kindness toward his sister. The only girl in the immediate family, Betty Pelham seems to have been something of a beloved princess. In a few letters, John revealed his affection for her, once making her a plough for her flower garden and taking time during his West Point summer furloughs to teach her and all her little friends how to ride horses. He corresponded with young female cousins in the north during his West Point years, again revealing that he enjoyed female company and taking time to teach the girls to ride horses "like Cavalry officers." So far, details about Pelham's opinions or interactions with enslaved women have been nearly impossible to find. He grew up surrounded by enslaved women and girls and most likely held views consistent with other young white southern males; whether he physically or sexually imposed on enslaved females at any time during his life is unknown, and without evidence, implications should not be made.

A brother's recollections hinted that John Pelham's romantic life was being pre-determined while he was still a boy. "My Mother & Mrs. Bush and the negroes had arranged it for two of the Pelham boys to marry the Bush girls and for Benton Bush to marry our only sister." Those fond maternal hopes came to nothing, and Pelham headed to West Point in 1856 at age 17. Around the time he departed, his older brother told a bunch of hospitable girls not to bother inviting John to leave the carriage for a short visit. "Ask him in? What's the use? Save your manners—he'd rather face the U.S. Army than a girl. He's the bashfulest fool—excuse me—about the girls you ever saw."

Pelham's shyness may have been lessened when away from his bold brothers and as he got older. During his five years at West Point, Pelham's surviving letters preserve some interesting changes in his thinking. One particular letter penned to a brother immediately after his furlough visit to Alabama during the summer of 1858 contains some regrets and advice that seems a mix of serious and tongue-in-cheek as he wrote about romance:

> But remember the best weapon for conquering woman is flattery. Don't talk to them about History or Grammar, nor the Phylosophy[sp] of Socrates, Plato or Zeno, but tell them about the Moon, spoons, the Starry Heavens, moonlight walks &c. flatter them, and be certain and let all your words be sentimental. I would like to be back in Ala again, although I am almost a follower of Machiavelli. . . . How & where

are Misses Henrietta Bush "Henrietta Robinson" & last but not least of all, Miss Addie. If she was sincere in what she said (but I don't believe she was) I have wronged her in telling her such lies—I respected her, liked her company, but to love a lady is not in my composition, now. I may outgrow my prejudices & my heart may become susceptible to the impressions of 'Woman's wiles, woman's smiles and woman's blandishments.' I would like so much to spend a few more short days in Calhoun [County]. Furlough seems like a pleasant dream, in which every action, word & thought is vividly stamped upon the mind, but thanks to the presiding Deity of the heart it has made no impression there. But that pleasant dream is past. I now stand face to face with the stern realities of life.

The youngest Pelham sibling and the only girl—Betty Pelham—liked gardening and horses, and her brother John encouraged her in both pursuits. After his death, she preserved his letters for many years. (jpha)

Clearly, John Pelham had learned how to talk to young women. He tried to focus on his military studies but also found time for social interactions. By 1859, he was organizing a concert evening for the Dialectic Society and told his mother that "I sometimes amuse myself by observing them [young ladies] with a small telescope as they are passing about." Still, he said he had not spoken to a lady since his furlough and "Think I will make a good Batchelor." However, a few weeks later he told a brother that he enjoyed meeting a family from Alabama and "I don't know what condition I might have been left in if one [of the girls] had remained a few days longer."

Pelham's interest in young women seems to have been tempered with realities. In December 1859, attending a wedding at the West Point chapel prompted him to tell his father, "Rather early to take a companion! I think a young officer ought to play his hand alone for four or five years at least after graduating. He ought to rough it on the frontiers for several years and learn whether Fate is propitious and in what direction Fortune showers her favors. That is the road I'll take." The following year, he called on some visiting acquaintances and helped to host the summer dances, acting as floor manager.

Secession and his decision to leave West Point consumed Pelham's thoughts, but he did contemplate marriage again around the time of his brother Charles's wedding. "Sister [Betty] is almost crazy about her [sister-in-law]—it is the first she has ever had. I think it would be doing her a kind and brotherly

Belle Boyd may have had a crush on Pelham in 1861, but she wrote a poetic line suggesting she knew he had affections for someone else. (loc)

Sarah "Sallie" Pendleton Dandridge may have had a serious relationship with John Pelham or they may have even been engaged. Family stories differ and primary source evidence either way has been inconclusive so far. (loc)

act to present her with another, but none of the girls will have me. It is the most unaccountable thing I ever heard of—don't you agree?" He also joked (or perhaps was serious) that he planned to befriend as many girls as possible so they would come and visit him if he got arrested.

The Civil War years and lack of his own writings open the door for speculation about Pelham and the ladies. His early biographers associated his name with Belle Boyd, Sarah "Sallie" Pendleton Dandridge, Bessie Shackelford, Nannie Price, and the oft-repeated story of three girls who went into mourning when he died. From fragments of existing primary sources written in real time (trying to avoid sources created years after), were any of these young women part of a romance with the blond Alabamian?

Belle Boyd did inscribe a Bible to Pelham in November 1861 and included a rather lengthy poem. One part of the poem indicates that Boyd may have had affectionate feelings toward Pelham, but she knew he did not return her sentiments and had an interest in someone else since "I know thou art loved by another now, I know thou wilt ne'er be mine. . . ." No other strong indication exists of a friendship or relationship between the two, and taken alone, this suggests a one-sided interest from the young woman.

Nannie Price, a distant relative of Gen. J. E. B. Stuart, interacted with Pelham and other officers, enjoying the fun and evening entertainments that occurred when the cavalry headquarters camped near her family's home in Hanover County. Some biographers have suggested an interest supposedly strengthened by one note that Price sent to Stuart in March 1863. She included some candy from "the little candy stew" adding that a friend named "Miss Brill" sent some candy for "the 'Gallant Pelham,' which you must be sure to give to him." Some biographers have suggested that a visit to Orange Court House to see Price and Brill started the chain of events that led to Pelham's arrival on the battlefield of Kelly's Ford. Pelham's interactions with Price seem to have been social and through Stuart's instigations. Miss Brill is still a mystery character, though some genealogical research suggests she may have lived in the lower Shenandoah Valley or Martinsburg area.

Sarah "Sallie" Pendleton Dandridge was the daughter of Adam Stephen Dandridge and lived at

"The Bower." (See Chapter 11). Stuart encamped the cavalry around this stately home for several weeks in the autumn of 1862. Fellow officers strongly hinted in their post-war writings that Pelham had some sort of romance with Sallie Dandridge, but did not reveal details or confirm her name in their public writings; however, biographers and fiction writers took the bait and launched the story to new levels. "The Bower" is undoubtedly a romantic setting, and it is easy to understand the draw to create a fast-paced romance for the "Gallant." More likely, but still conjecture, Pelham met Dandridge during the summer of 1861 and formed some sort of attachment. Some of Pelham's relatives recalled that Atkinson Pelham and Stephen

"The Bower" was where military friends thought Pelham spent some of the happiest days of his life during the war years. (skb)

William Pegram—another young Confederate artillerist—was alarmed to hear rumors that he was engaged to young women he was barely acquainted with. Apparently, some single women thought it was fashionable to claim an engagement with a Confederate officer. (loc)

Dandridge exchanged cordial letters, something that socially would have been expected after a lengthier acquaintance as a couple moved toward engagement and marriage. (Other relatives stoutly insisted that Pelham had no romantic attachments at all.)

The best evidence for a romantic attachment between John Pelham and Sallie Dandridge exists in her cousin's writings. John E. Cooke—staff officer with Stuart, cousin of Stuart's wife, and relative of the Dandridge's of "The Bower"—wrote a lot of historical fiction in the post-war era, including pieces about Pelham. However, his war era letters seem to have more facts. Hearing of Pelham's death in March 1863, Cooke wrote, "His death was a heavy blow to me, and will be to Sal. I don't think they were engaged." Then, nearly a year later, Cooke clearly had more knowledge of his relative's feelings and said that there had been an engagement between Pelham and Dandridge. Some stories suggest that Sallie Dandridge may have been present at Pelham's funeral in Richmond; if true, she could not have traveled from "The Bower" to Richmond in time, which raises the question if she was already in Richmond or a nearby town. Pelham seemed to have had some anxiety about getting away from cavalry headquarters during the winter of 1862-1863, but whether that was to see his fiancée, or for other reasons, is not known. If there was an engagement (or soon to be an engagement), it seems to have been a family secret. Given Stuart's merciless teasing or the no-man's-land position of the Dandridge family home, it is not out of historical context that there could have been a personal or even military reason to keep a relationship secret.

Bessie Shackelford lived with her family in Culpeper, Virginia. She and Pelham were socially acquainted and spent winter evenings in the parlor of the Shackelford home in early 1863. When Pelham was mortally wounded at Kelly's Ford, he was eventually transported to that home where he died in the early morning hours of March 18, 1863. Biographers and novelists have firmly created a romance between Pelham and Shackelford, choosing to either ignore Dandridge or suggesting a break-up or love triangle. Evidence of romance in Culpeper is historically weak, but proof of normal 19th century social interactions is strong. Shackelford talked warmly about Pelham in an interview, remembering that he was a good dance partner and that they spent quite a bit of time talking together, but she referred to him as "a boy, a splendid boy." According to some sources, Pelham told someone that Bessie reminded him of his sister. Both Pelham's lack of interest to spend extended time in Culpeper, the possible family comment, and the slight trivializing in Bessie's words, suggest a platonic friendship.

What about the persistent story that at least three girls put on mourning for Pelham after he died? It appears in countless articles, but has little evidence that it actually happened or any clarification about what is meant by the comment. Generally, it is written as evidence that Pelham had multiple romantic attachments. However, socially, men and women could wear mourning for public figures without family or romantic interest—as evidenced at "Stonewall" Jackson funeral and Lincoln's funeral, along with many others.

Additionally, since Pelham died unmarried and not engaged (at least as far as the public knew), he could have been an easy target for desperate young women. The idea is not socially a stretch. Another bachelor Confederate artillerist, Willie Pegram, found himself the victim of rumors in Richmond from several young ladies who claimed that he was in love with them. Having barely met these women, Pegram was very disturbed by the gossip and offended at the implications for both his romantic choices and his honor. If girls were doing that while an officer was alive, how easy would it have been to tell a story and put on formal mourning if the famous bachelor officer was already dead?

After the war's end, Pelham's legacy got no rest from romantic rumors and twists. But why? What was the draw to inventing love stories, flirtations, or affairs for him? The Lost Cause. This ideology rapidly adopted Pelham into the pantheon of Confederate heroes. As the viewpoint evolved to make those heroes the icons of white southern manhood, Pelham, in real life, had to be conformed to Pelham of myths. His life could check most of the boxes: handsome, courageous, supporter of secession, and battlefield victories. However, the usually unspoken part of the Lost Cause ideology is white patriarchy which is tied to sexual prowess. Since Pelham was a bachelor and sex outside of marriage was taboo (even

Pelham's life, death, and memory are a chance to reflect on what historical memory does to person's story . . . and why. (skb)

though it happened), the Lost Cause needed "parlor conquests." They needed Pelham to be "the greatest flirt that ever lived"—whether he was or not. They needed the stories of love triangles and young women in mourning. They needed stories about girls to *make* their hero. Biographers—especially William Hassler (1960), who continues to be extensively sourced and quoted—have made Pelham the figure slipping into shrubberies with girls, quickly abandoning Sallie in favor of Bessie, and spending excessive amounts of unchaperoned time with young women.

How would Pelham have felt about the implications of this part of the Lost Cause? Two strong suggestions lie in primary sources. First, his West Point letter of September 1859 expressed some measure of regret if he had led a girl on. Second, a cavalryman hinted at a level of sexual innocence when he recorded: "I recall an incident once, while gathered around a campfire, another cavalryman told an off-color story that caused Pelham to blush like a girl." Pelham may have enjoyed some aspects of his Lost Cause legacy, but the excessive interest in him as a romantic figure would likely have made him at least somewhat uncomfortable.

In a letter to his mother written from West Point in 1860, Pelham showed his feelings about rumors and the incident of a normal social visit at one of the academy's formal gathering places:

> *I passed a very pleasant time last Saturday afternoon. I mention it because it is such an uncommon thing for me to call on ladies—in fact it is the first time I have done so since I left camp. I felt very awkward, particularly when I started—for about twenty Cadets commenced hollowing 'Look here fellows Pelham has turn lady's man—he is going to make calls—John is getting spoony—he is going to the Hotel' etc., etc. directly another crowd took it up and then another & another, until there was at least 100 or 150 hollowing at me. They never hollowed at anybody else, they think as a matter of course everybody but myself can go—in fact there were three other Cadets going to call on ladies at the hotel with me, but no one said anything to them,— they thought they had a right to go. And didn't I have a right? Yes, an imperative duty—for a very particular friend from Newburg had been on the Point almost a week and I had not called on her. (Emphasis added.)*

Pelham had an interest in girls, but whether he actually fell in love or seriously pursued a romantic relationship of any sort is simply not clearly known.

The myths recall their versions of stories, but in the end, the feelings of a man's heart are his own unless he shares them. No one has a right to force this excessive speculation into Pelham's possible relationship interests. In this respect, the Lost Cause has been invasively unfair to Pelham, and it has also used the girls connected to his life in a careless, patriarchal way to further its hero image.

"How shall we rank thee
upon glorys page
Than more than Soldier

This inscription on Pelham's grave monument hints at the glory stories that surround both Custer and Pelham in historical memory. (skb)

West Point Classmates
John Pelham and George A. Custer

APPENDIX B
BY DANIEL T. DAVIS

They hailed from different walks of life. George Armstrong Custer came from the small hamlet of New Rumley, Ohio. His father, Emmanuel, made a living as the village blacksmith. Emmanuel introduced "Autie," a nickname for the young Custer, to the military while a member of the local militia company. Autie spent his childhood between Ohio and with his half-sister, Ann, and her husband in Monroe, Michigan, which eventually became his adopted hometown.

Custer's beginning greatly contrasted with John Pelham. Pelham entered the world of the Alabama planter class. Born on a farm in modern Calhoun County, Pelham's father was a doctor and owned several large properties. While Pelham arguably enjoyed a more comfortable childhood, both he and Custer grew up in a house filled with rambunctious siblings. Two of Custer's brothers later fell with him at the Little Bighorn.

Their trails crossed in the summer of 1856 as both Custer and Pelham entered the United States Military Academy at West Point. Although Custer came from a family of Jacksonian Democrats and his politics placed him in line with beliefs of many Southerners, his outgoing personality allowed him to easily move amongst his fellow cadets. He counted many friends, both North and South, including Pelham.

The rigid discipline and demanding courses at the academy formed a shared bond among the cadets. That bond was tested as the country quickly spiraled toward Civil War. Unlike fellow cadets Emory Upton and Wade Hampton Gibbs, whose views over slavery led to fisticuffs, Custer and Pelham seemingly never

George Custer attended West Point and graduated in the Class of (June) 1861, making him one year behind Pelham at the academy. (loc)

Historical memory paints both Custer and Pelham as flamboyant and daring. (loc)

allowed their differences to impact their relationship. Still, while Custer could turn a blind eye to slavery, he could never tolerate the dissolution of the Union.

The 1860 election of Abraham Lincoln and the secession of several Southern states to form the Confederate States of America accelerated the tension at West Point. On April 12, 1861, Confederate forces fired on Fort Sumter in Charleston Harbor. This event forced Pelham's hand. Ten days later, Pelham, along with Thomas L. Rosser, another close friend of Custer's, resigned from the academy to offer their services to their Confederacy. There, Custer and Pelham's trails diverged. They would cross only one more time.

Pelham's star in the Confederate army rose almost immediately. He emerged as the skillful leader of the horse artillery attached to Maj. Gen. J. E. B. Stuart's cavalry in the Army of Northern Virginia. Custer fought at First Manassas with the 2nd U.S. Cavalry and through the first two years of the conflict, moved from one staff position to another. While Pelham distinguished himself at Antietam in September 1862 atop Nicodemus Heights, Custer served as an aide to the commander of the Army of the Potomac, Maj. Gen. George McClellan.

Pelham's finest hour came at the Battle of Fredericksburg on December 13, 1862. About mid-morning, Pelham positioned a single gun on the Union right flank and opened fire. For the better part of an hour, his barrage delayed the advance of two Federal divisions. Pelham finally withdrew only after losing a piece sent to support him and running low on ammunition. His star was extinguished on St. Patrick's Day, 1863, at the Battle of Kelly's Ford.

As the light from Pelham's star faded, Custer's began to rise. A little over three months later, Custer received a promotion to brigadier general and command of four regiments of Michigan cavalry. His hours of greatness came repeatedly until the end of the war at Gettysburg, Meadow Bridge, Haw's Shop, Cold Harbor, Cedar Creek, Waynesboro and Appomattox. One of his troopers mortally wounded Pelham's mentor and former commander, Jeb Stuart, at Yellow Tavern. Custer ended the conflict as a brevet major general of volunteers. At Tom's Brook in October 1864, Custer took on and thoroughly

Custer was known to renew acquaintances with former friends who had joined the Confederacy's ranks. There is a story that Custer sent Pelham a note across the lines after the battle of Fredericksburg, but the two former friends' locations in the winter of 1862 cast some doubt on the story. (loc)

defeated a division commanded by Pelham's former West Point roommate, Thomas Rosser.

After the war, Custer received a commission as lieutenant colonel in the newly instated 7th U.S. Cavalry. He endured a court martial conviction in 1867 and returned to lead his regiment in successful campaigns against the Southern Cheyenne. Custer participated in the 1873 Yellowstone Expedition, where he rekindled his old academy friendship with Rosser, and the 1874 Black Hills Expedition. Surviving the entanglement of a political controversy related to the U.S. Grant administration, Custer rode out from Fort Abraham Lincoln in Dakota Territory at the head of his regiment against the Sioux and Northern Cheyenne on May 17, 1876.

George Custer survived the Civil War and held the rank of major general by age 25. (loc)

Custer and Pelham's trails crossed again, in death. Both their passings are clouded in mystery, a mystery that continues to cloud with the passage of time. On March 17, 1863, Union cavalry under Brig. Gen. William W. Averell crossed the Rappahannock River at Kelly's Ford to engage Confederates under Brig. Gen. Fitzhugh Lee. Pelham, several miles away at Culpeper Court House, rode out to join Lee. During an advance against Averell's right, a shell burst above Pelham, sending a piece of shrapnel into Pelham's neck. Taken to a house in Culpeper, he died the next day. No one saw Pelham fall, and the accounts related to his mortal wounding do not agree in detail.

In pursuit of a village under Sitting Bull and Crazy Horse, Custer and five companies from the Seventh, met death on the east bank of the Little Bighorn River in southwest Montana Territory on June 25, 1876. While Pelham's death became footnote to the ascending dominance of the Union cavalry in the Eastern Theater, Custer's became one of the mythic moments in the story of the American West. Custer's death also served as a catalyst. His defeat marked a mobilization of the U.S. Army not seen since the Civil War, as regiments from various western departments converged on the Northern Plains for the subjugation of the Sioux. Eleven months later, Crazy Horse surrendered and Sitting Bull eventually fled to Canada.

Pelham's sudden death at Kelly's Ford opens the door for some of the continuing comparisons between Custer and Pelham: both attended West Point, both fought gallantly in the Civil War and rose rapidly in rank, and both had sudden battlefield deaths.
(loc)

GENERAL CUSTER'S DEATH STRUGGLE.
The Battle of the Little Big Horn

While some aspects of Custer's death were provided by members of the burial party and the final maneuvers by subsequent archeology at the Little Bighorn, like Pelham, the specifics will remain elusive for the time being. We will never fully know, until, as James Kidd, a former officer in Custer's Michigan Brigade wrote "until the dead are called upon to give up their secrets."

Custer met a violent death in the battle of Little Bighorn in 1876. (loc)

DANIEL T. DAVIS *is the Senior Education Manager at the American Battlefield Trust. A native of Fredericksburg, VA, he has authored or co-authored numerous books and articles, including a short biography of George Custer.*

Pelham's Corner preserves land and the story of the Alabamian's fight at Fredericksburg in December 1862. (skb)

Saving Pelham's Corner

"The preservation of an iconic part of the Fredericksburg battlefield"

APPENDIX C
By Thomas Van Winkle

When leaders plan a battle, sometimes, actually more often than not, the initial strategy does not hold up after the first shot is fired. The mission of preserving our Civil War battlefields often parallels this scenario, and so it was with saving "Pelham's Corner."

The Central Virginia Battlefields Trust (CVBT) was formed in 1996. The mission of the Central Virginia Battlefields Trust is "to preserve land associated with the four major campaigns: Fredericksburg, Chancellorsville, Mine Run, and the Overland Campaign, including the Wilderness and Spotsylvania." As of the writing of this publication, CVBT has saved nearly 2,000 acres of battlefields otherwise lost forever.

The CVBT had been attempting to purchase the parcel located at the corner of Benchmark Road and Tidewater trail, modern day route 608 and U.S. 17/Virginia Highway 2, that is now known as "Pelham's Corner" for quite some time, but to no avail. The owners were determined to build a commercial development on the historic corner.

In 1999, CVBT changed strategies, much like in the heat of battle, and pivoted to two properties close by the desired corner. Neither of these lots held any special historic significance, but it was thought maybe they would play into the needs of the developer in the future.

Central Virginia Battlefields Trust

The Central Virginia Battlefields Trust has been preserving land at Fredericksburg, Chancellorsville, the Wilderness, and Spotsylvania Court House since 1996. (cvbt)

Here, Pelham insisted on staying in his advanced position until he was out of ammunition . . . and Union infantry began advancing on his hideout. (skb)

In August 1999, CVBT purchased the first lot totaling .3 acres for $8,000. This property was just a few hundred feet from the corner. In January 2000, CVBT then acquired a second parcel .33 acres in size and next to the previous lot for a cost of $10,500.

Again, neither of these parcels held any historic significance, but CVBT was playing chess here, not checkers.

The Silver Companies, one of the area's largest local developers, purchased the corner and remaining land in and around CVBT's newly owned property. The company then formed a subsidiary called "Pelhams Corner LLC." and intended to develop the area.

CVBT had worked with the Silver Company before with success, so we approached them touting the importance of the corner and its great historic value. Unfortunately, CVBT did not have the financial means in which to meet the purchase price of the property in question.

Then, in 2004, another move was made in the game of chess. In order to develop the area commercially and build what was then a large pharmacy store, the Silver Company required additional acreage behind the proposed building. Yes, the very land CVBT had purchased in 1999 and 2000. So, a land swap deal was initiated giving the developer the acreage they needed

to build and CVBT the desired historical corner where the "Gallant Pelham" had frustrated the Union assault on Slaughter Pen farm with one remaining cannon.

In 2004, the two lots CVBT paid a total of $18,500 appraised for $130,000. The corner property, of .972 acres, traded for these two parcels, then appraised for 1.185 million dollars. The land swap was completed, and the historic corner was then preserved in perpetuity.

Included in this agreement, the Silver Company also contributed $10,000 for landscaping and interpretation. Several dedicated parking spaces were also deeded to CVBT.

Now owning this historic property, CVBT set out to interpret the site so the public could learn of the heroics that occurred here in December 1862. The property already included a stone marker. The marker was one of several stones placed around the battlefields in 1903 by the Reverend James Power Smith, a Fredericksburg resident and a lieutenant on Gen. "Stonewall" Jackson's staff.

The marker is eighteen inches square, two feet two inches tall and reads:

Stuart and Pelham
Battle of Fredericksburg
Dec. 13, 1862

The small tract of land preserved at Pelham's Corner offers a chance to stand where history happened. (skb)

Pelham credited his officers and men for their courage at Fredericksburg, seeming uncomfortable or overwhelmed by the accolades he received after the battle. (skb)

CVBT improved the marker location by unearthing it, building a stone protective pedestal and replacing it in the same position as it was originally. This protects the original stone from mowing and other land maintenance.

The site still did not exude the merited appearance. In July 2013, CVBT decided the location truly needed a cannon. The cannon was fabricated by Steen Cannon and Ordnance Works, a nationally known manufacturer. The cost of the cannon was approximately $19,500. Not wanting to spend our members' donations on items other than battlefield land, CVBT embarked on a funding plan with like-minded entities.

CVBT received a grant of $6,000 from the Duff McDuff Green, Jr. Fund of the Community Foundation of the Rappahannock River Region. CVBT also received $9,900 from The Blue & Gray Education Society, one of the premier Civil War education organizations in the country. Rounding out the donations one of CVBT 's members, and most ardent supporters, James W. Davis, donated $3,300. The cannon is an exact replica of the twelve-pound Napoleon Pelham had used.

The story has not yet concluded. In September 2015, after the Silver Companies had finished developing the area, they gifted CVBT an additional three parcels, now making CVBT's holdings nearly 4.5 acres including the historic corner.

Today, a lone cannon sits sentinel over a place where one of the Civil Wars most remarkable feats of courage and tenacity occurred. Even when a battle plan starts without much hope, re-strategizing can make all the difference.

THOMAS VAN WINKLE *is the President of the Central Virginia Battlefields Trust. He has been instrumental in saving battlefield land at Fredericksburg, Chancellorsville, the Wilderness, and Spotsylvania Court House and has authored numerous articles.*

Suggested Reading

GLORIOUS COURAGE

The Perfect Lion: The Life and Death of Confederate Artillerist John Pelham
Jerry H. Maxwell
University Alabama Press, 2011
ISBN: 978-0817317355

Looking for a longer biography about John Pelham? This one is the best for an in-depth look at the artillerist's life and the details of his battle tactics. Maxwell's endnotes also provide valuable insight to the ongoing mystery of Pelham's lost letters and the long historiography and memory around his life and death.

Gallant Pelham: American Extraordinary
Charles G. Milham
Public Affairs Press, 1959
ISBN: 978-0942211634
Though published in the mid-20th century and heavy with hero worship and the Lost Cause, Milham's biography of "Gallant Pelham" offers some unique perspectives from eyewitnesses that are difficult to find or cite in other sources. Milham spent decades in the early part of his life researching, traveling, and interviewing eyewitnesses or their children for Civil War accounts about Pelham, and he was recognized by peers for his careful and dedicated research.

The Myth of the Lost Cause and Civil War History
Gary W. Gallagher and Alan T. Nolan (editors)
Indiana University Press, 2000
ISBN: 978-0253222664
This collection of essays examines the rise of the Confederate Lost Cause and its hallmarks of thought. Though Pelham is not the subject of an essay, many of his contemporaries are mentioned. The book is a helpful groundwork for examining the effects of the Lost Cause on Civil War history and thought-provoking for considering how historical figures have been viewed over the years.

With Pen & Saber: The letters and diaries of J. E. B. Stuart's Staff Officers
Robert J. Trout
Stackpole Books, 1995
ISBN: 978-0811719308
John Pelham was not officially on Stuart's staff, but he was usually present at cavalry headquarters and knew most of the officers. These primary sources have occasional mentions of Pelham and are also helpful for noting the culture of the Confederate cavalry in Virginia and the military/social norms frequently practiced.

Galloping Thunder: The Stuart Horse Artillery Battalion
Robert J. Trout
Stackpole Books, 2002
ISBN: 978-0811707077
This is a must-read book for learning more about horse artillery tactics and the organization and battles of the Stuart Horse Artillery. While helpful for studying the years that Pelham was in command, the book goes beyond March 1863 and traces the unit's history through the last campaigns of the Civil War.

Memoirs of the Confederate War for Independence
Heros Von Borcke
J. P. Lippincott & Co., 1867
[No ISBN at the time of original printing; there are many reprints.]
This lively memoir probably stretches the truth and fills in memory's blanks with extra color, but Heros Von Borcke experienced the American Civil War as a member of Stuart's staff. Von Borcke and Pelham seemed to have been friends and had many adventures.

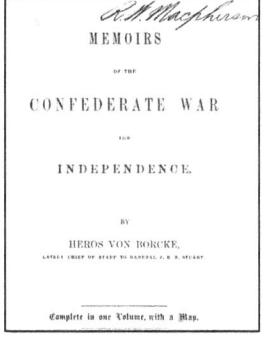

Blood Image: Turner Ashby in the Civil War and the Southern Mind
Paul Christopher Anderson
Louisiana State University Press, 2002
ISBN: 978-0807131619
Turner Ashby—a Confederate cavalry commander in the Shenandoah Valley—died in June 1862 and became a Confederate symbol of chivalry and martyrdom. While this book examines Ashby's life and his role in the 1862 Valley Campaign, it also delves deep into the southern mindset of chivalry, cavalry, and hero memory—making it an interesting study in comparison and contrast to Pelham's life and memory.

About the Author

Sarah Kay Bierle works in the public history field, focusing on education and battlefield preservation. A graduate from Thomas Edison State University with a B.A. in History, she has spent years researching, writing, and speaking about the American Civil War, helping audiences gain a stronger appreciation for the accounts of real people caught in the struggles of the past. She has written essays and several other books, including *Call Out The Cadets* in the Emerging Civil War Series.

Sarah's research interest in Pelham's life and memory started in 2018 while reading several biographies and working on a blog post for the Emerging Civil War. From gravel roads and grassy knolls to university libraries, icy afternoons at Kelly's Ford to a perfect spring sunset in Alabama, the next years took many twists and turns hunting for context and primary sources.

Currently, Sarah continues to research and hike battlefields, often studying military and civilian interactions or pausing to continue documenting lesser-known accounts in the Shenandoah Valley.